An **Eight-Cow**
*Woman*
Deserves an
**Eight-Cow**
*Man*

# Tracy Lyn Cutler
### with Kurt Dowdle and Ty B. Erickson, M.D.

# An **Eight-Cow**
# *Woman*
## Deserves an
# **Eight-Cow**
# *Man*

## Eight Critical Character Traits For
## A Meaningful Life and Fulfilling Relationships

Cache Valley Press, LLC

**Library of Congress Cataloging-in-Publication Data Upon Request**

ISBN 978-1-60641-733-1

Printed in the United States of America

10   9   8   7   6   5   4   3   2

*To our parents.*

# Contents

CONTENTS

# Acknowledgements

*I* gratefully acknowledge the countless individuals of character and courage who have inspired this book. I would especially like to thank my parents, grandparents, teachers, and other mentors whose lives are consistent with the precepts they teach. I have drawn many of my thoughts from their examples.

Thanks to Dr. Ty Erickson for his support, brilliant ideas, and encouragement. I would also like to thank Kurt Dowdle for helping me find my writing voice. Much of what is written here was a true collaboration.

Thanks as well go to Tonya Facemyer for typesetting, Richard Peterson for editing, Kayla Hackett for cover design, Dorothy Rackley for additional editing, and Jana Erickson for invaluable suggestions and encouragement.

Thanks also to the many people who responded to my surveys and questionnaires. Their input has been invaluable.

And lastly, I express my gratitude to my friends and family members who have been so supportive during this whole process.

—Tracy Lyn Cutler

# Johnny and Sarita

*A*n eight-cow woman deserves an eight-cow man. Many people immediately pick up on the obvious tie this statement has to the parable of Johnny Lingo. But if you have never heard the story of Johnny Lingo and his eight-cow bride, Sarita, then my title could be a little confusing. And considering that the ancient tradition of bartering for a wife is no longer a common practice in most countries, you may wonder about its relevance. You might even wonder about my rationality to make such a statement, but there is an important point here. And trust me, once you hear the story of Johnny Lingo, it will all start to make sense.

Johnny Lingo is the main character in a nineteenth-century tale set in the South Sea islands. It was written by Patricia McGerr in

1965 and first published in *Woman's Day Magazine*. Though set in the past, the parable of Johnny Lingo was written to address modern issues observed by the author.

I can't remember precisely the first time I heard the story of Johnny Lingo. I believe I was either ten or eleven years old. I know I heard the story in my Sunday School class, but I may have heard it first from my mother. I do remember I listened to the story with child-like fascination and tried to picture the tropical paradise of Kiniwata with its sandy beaches, lush foliage, palm trees, and ocean breezes. I was intrigued by the whole "cows for a wife" concept and the romantic notion of Johnny paying an exorbitant eight cows for the woman he loved when the going bride-price was only two or three cows.

Over the years the story has gained popularity and has been used as a great morality tale in lessons and sermons alike. It was reprinted in the February 1988 *Reader's Digest* and adapted for two different movies. Multiple variations of the story can also be found on literally hundreds, perhaps thousands of websites and blogs on the internet. If you haven't read it or if you have only seen the movies, it is definitely worth reading. For your convenience I will retell the story in my own words to the best of my recollection.

Johnny Lingo was the sharpest trader in the islands. Nobody it seemed could make a deal like Johnny. He was also single, young, handsome, and the heartthrob of every eligible maiden. He had recently announced he was returning to his home island, the beautiful tropical paradise of Kiniwata, to bargain for a bride. The whole island was abuzz with excitement.

Johnny could have had any woman he wanted in the entire South Pacific. So when it was rumored he had chosen to bargain for Sarita, the plainest girl on the island, people were shocked. They assumed the only logical reason for such a choice was because Johnny would be able to negotiate the price of his bride with Sarita's father, old Sam Karoo, down to the minimum price of only one cow . . . or less!

———•·•———

*As long as most people could remember, it had been the custom on Kiniwata for a young man to offer cows as payment for his bride.*

As long as most people could remember, it had been the custom on Kiniwata for a young man to offer cows as payment to his future father-in-law. Two cows were usually enough for an average wife. Three cows might acquire a reasonably pleasant looking woman while four cows could secure a spouse to be truly proud of.

———•·•———

The most ever paid was five cows—the price for a woman of exceptional beauty and charm. Each woman's value, and to a certain extent her self-esteem, was forever afterward measured by the number of cows she fetched at the marriage negotiation.

The statement, "I was a three-cow bride," could easily be

trumped by the proclamation, "Well my husband paid four cows for me!" And both women had to defer to the declaration, "My father demanded five cows from my husband." In these social contests, however, the two-cow women usually stayed quiet.

The marriage negotiation was traditionally held in front of the father's hut and was often as entertaining as an athletic event. Sometimes the whole village would gather around to eavesdrop as the father of the maiden and her suitor would sit face-to-face and haggle over the number of cows the father required for the hand of his daughter. Since it was considered a sacrifice for a father to give up his daughter, it was expected he would seek as many cows as he could get as compensation for his loss. The joke had circulated for quite some time that Sam could probably be convinced to let his daughter Sarita go for just the horns and a hoof.

Sarita was extremely shy and liked to cling to the shadows. But she worked hard for her widowed father. She was sensitive to his pain and loneliness even though he ignored hers. She tried to cook pleasant meals and keep their hut nice and comfortable. Her father was very disappointed, however, that she did little to make herself appealing to any of the young men in the village. And he felt a little bitter that she probably wouldn't bring much of a price at any marriage negotiation, even if anyone did show an interest in her.

Consequently, Sam Karoo was stunned when he heard that the legendary Johnny Lingo had come to Kiniwata to bargain for his daughter, Sarita. He was as confused as everyone else in the village. Why would he want to bargain for Sarita? Particularly when coming up with five cows for a superior wife shouldn't pose a problem for the great Johnny Lingo.

Sam wasn't about to question the reasons. He started to plan his future with new hope. Let's see . . . Johnny could easily pay five cows for a bride—but how much would he be willing to pay for Sarita? His brother had suggested that if he asked Johnny for three cows he might get at least one cow out of the deal. But the people of the village also might laugh him to scorn if he asked such a high price for such a homely daughter. Sam's newfound hope was waning. How could he possibly out-negotiate Johnny Lingo? As the sun began to set on the day before the negotiation, Sam was even more nervous than before.

The sun shone bright on the morning of the bargaining ceremony. On his way to meet with Sarita's father, Johnny Lingo stopped in to see his friend Shenkin, a local shop owner and trader. Shenkin was originally from Chicago. He had come to Kiniwata just after the American Civil War and had been a successful trader on the island for nearly thirty years. He was the man responsible for Johnny's Americanized name and had taught Johnny everything he knew about business and the art of trading. But Johnny's skill in business had long-since surpassed Shenkin's.

Shenkin, in a playful voice spoke first, "So, Johnny, I hear you are bargaining with old Sam Karoo for Sarita today."

"Yes. It will be the most important deal I will make in my life," Johnny said in a more serious tone.

Sensing Johnny's pensive mood, Shenkin became even more curious about Johnny's intentions. "Johnny, it is none of my business why you would want to bargain for the plainest girl in the islands, but it should be the easiest deal you'll ever make. You don't have competition for Sarita and Sam is pretty much willing to take anything you offer—just to have her off his hands. What's the problem?"

*"I didn't say it was going to be my most difficult deal," Johnny chided, "I said it would be my most important."*

"I didn't say it was going to be my most difficult deal," Johnny chided, "I said it would be my most important. But I don't have time to chat right now—here is an order for a gift I am buying for Sarita. I need to have it delivered to my home on the island of Nurabandi."

"This is a very expensive item," Shenkin cautioned, "It could take quite some time to get it here."

"That's okay," Johnny replied, "We will be honeymooning for quite awhile. You can even bring it yourself, if you would like."

Sam Karoo waited nervously in front of his hut. Johnny isn't going to show up, he thought. This is nothing but a cruel joke. Why would anyone want Sarita? Johnny hasn't seen her for quite some time now. Perhaps he has forgotten just how ugly she really is. Sarita hadn't been seen all day long. Maybe that was a good thing. One look at her and the deal would definitely be off.

Sam heard a rustling in the undergrowth and soon Johnny emerged. It looked as though the whole island was following him. This was going to be embarrassing. Now everyone was going to witness his shame. Maybe he should just give her to Johnny for nothing and get the whole thing over with.

Johnny opened the bargaining ritual by calling out, "I seek the father of Sarita!" Sam responded in the traditional reply, "I am the father of Sarita." As was the custom, Johnny and Sam sat on the ground in front of Sam's hut and began the negotiation.

Johnny and Sam faced each other and began to recite several customary phrases that basically say, "I want to marry your daughter," followed by, "Giving up my daughter will be such a burden—it's going to be hard to say good-bye and she is such a comfort to me, blah, blah, blah . . ." The longer the father rants about his sacrifice, the more cows he is bound to ask for his daughter.

Sam didn't rant much at all. He mumbled something about how she didn't burn the fish that often and that she was pretty good at thatching a roof. He then waited for Johnny to recite the customary phrase, "I understand the love a father must have for his daughter. I promise to love her as well—I am willing to pay for your sacrifice. What is your price for Sarita?"

Sam sensed every eye upon him as the village waited in silent suspense for his response. No matter what happens, he thought, this will be the most embarrassing moment of my life. He could feel his face flush. He wanted to die right there. He was feeling faint . . . Then Sam had an epiphany! He realized  he was a man with nothing to lose. Acting impulsively for the first time in his life, Sam blurted out, "I seek FIVE COWS for my Sarita!"

People couldn't believe their ears. Had they heard right? Five cows—the maximum price? A roar of laughter burst from the gathering of onlookers. Sam tried to ignore them and stared at Johnny, waiting for his counter-offer. He had already decided that no matter how low it was, he would accept it and end this spectacle.

Johnny motioned for the throng to be silent then said thoughtfully:

"Five cows is many, but . . ."

Johnny paused. Everyone waited. Sam dared not look around and continued to stare ahead. Time stood still.

" . . . but not enough for my Sarita. I offer you EIGHT COWS and nothing less."

The crowd went wild!

Johnny immediately stood and extended his hand to seal the deal. Sam rose, dazed and confused, and offered a limp handshake in return. The people who had gathered around laughed hysterically. They couldn't make sense of it all. Sam Karoo had instantly become one of the richest men on the island, and plain old Sarita was betrothed to the most handsome, well-off bachelor ever—for the unprecedented price of eight cows! It was unbelievable.

Johnny knew this kind of attention would make Sarita very uncomfortable. He put his arm around his future father-in-law and spoke directly in his ear. He arranged for immediate delivery of the eight cows and demanded a private wedding ceremony within the hour. That was the last the people of Kiniwata would see of Johnny and Sarita for quite some time.

*First he pays eight cows for Sarita and then he buys the homeliest girl in the islands a mirror?*

Several months had passed when Johnny's gift for Sarita arrived at Shenkin's store. It was heavy for its size. Shenkin opened it for inspection. He examined it carefully—it was an ornate sterling silver hand mirror highlighted with gold and precious stones. "This must have cost Johnny half his fortune," he thought. He contemplated the irony of the gift. A mirror—for Sarita. What was Johnny thinking? "Oh, well," he mused. "Johnny always was very unconventional."

Shenkin remembered that Johnny had invited him to deliver the gift in person. It had been a while since he had visited the island of Nurabandi. Maybe he could get to the bottom of his friend's mysterious behavior. First he pays eight cows for Sarita and then he buys the homeliest girl in the islands a mirror? He needed an explanation. He boxed the gift back up and then got ready for the half-day boat trip.

When Shenkin was in sight of Johnny's residence, Johnny immediately ran into the courtyard to greet him.

"I am so glad to see you, my old friend," Johnny beamed.

Shenkin returned the greeting as they threw their arms around each other.

"I see you have brought Sarita's gift. May I see it?" Johnny asked.

Johnny examined the mirror. "I am so pleased. It is as beautiful as I imagined. Sarita will be very surprised."

"Surprised indeed," Shenkin shot back with an almost accusatory air.

Johnny raised an eyebrow, "I see you have brought with you something more than Sarita's gift. You also come bearing questions. Come into my home and you may ask them."

As they sat down in Johnny's spacious dwelling, Johnny spoke first. "You want to know about the eight cows," he stated.

Shenkin stammered, "Well, sure. Who doesn't?"

"They still talk about it on Kiniwata?" Johnny asked.

"Yes. Practically every day."

"They do here on Nurabandi, as well. Perhaps there isn't an

island anywhere that hasn't heard at least one of several versions of the event. But think of it Shenkin—" Johnny's chest expanded with satisfaction, "Always and forever, when they speak of marriage settlements, it will be remembered that Johnny Lingo paid eight cows for Sarita."

"That's it," Shenkin thought. "Vanity. Nothing but vanity."

Then he saw her . . .

The most striking woman he had ever seen glided into the room and quietly placed two cool drinks on the table.

"Shenkin, you remember my wife Sarita from Kiniwata?" Johnny offered politely.

Shenkin mumbled something that resembled a greeting and continued to stare. Everything about this woman bespoke elegance and grace; the way she moved, the tilt of her chin, the way she walked. Shenkin was in a trance. Sarita then left the two men to continue their discussion.

Shenkin closed his gaping mouth. "That was Sarita?" he asked.

A smile came over Johnny's lips, "Do you think eight cows were too many for such a woman?"

"No!" Shenkin replied. "She is magnificent. But I don't understand; how can she be so different?"

"Do you ever think," Johnny asked, "what it must mean to a woman to know that her husband bargained to obtain her for the fewest cows possible? And when the women talk, how does the two-cow bride feel when others brag of being purchased for four cows or five? This could not happen to my Sarita!"

"So you did this to make Sarita happy?"

"Yes. I wanted her to be happy. But I wanted more than that. Many things can change a woman, or any person for that matter— things that happen on the inside and things that happen on the outside. But the thing that matters most is what you think of yourself."

"On Kiniwata, because of the way her father and others treated her, Sarita believed she was worth nothing. Just like this mirror, she began to reflect those beliefs. But I have always known Sarita was beautiful. I was honored to offer eight cows for her. And in this house she now knows she is worth more than any other woman in the islands."

"Then you wanted—"

"I wanted to marry Sarita. I have loved her since I was young and no other woman. But that wasn't enough."

Shenkin was finally beginning to understand.

"You see," Johnny finished softly, "I wanted an eight-cow wife."

<hr />

Isn't that romantic? Well, I think it is, in a quirky, nineteenth-century sort of way. But now that I am grown and have learned a thing or two about the sometimes harsh realities of life, I read this story with a different perspective. Now, as I think of Johnny and

Sarita, I see beyond the fantasies of tropical islands and romantic gestures and yearn to address and solve practical aspects of life and relationships.

I often wonder if there's a way to stop or even slow down the continual drifting apart of modern-day Johnny and Sarita. And what is the secret, if there is one, to a long life of bliss where a man and a woman raise a happy family and then grow old together under the same thatched roof? That is why I am writing this book. I believe there's an answer to these questions and concerns. But I don't think it's discovering a secret as much as it may be just paying attention to important principles that too many of us overlook.

*Isn't that romantic? Well, I think it is, in a quirky, nineteenth-century sort of way.*

These principles are not new—they are timeless. I present them here in what I hope is a unique and engaging setting that will aid in better understanding. And it doesn't matter if you are in your early teens—just beginning to explore the mysteries of a relationship—or in your later years— trying to hold onto the vestiges of a tired marriage. The principles are the same.

I will admit that the title of this book was the first thing that came to me. I was thinking about a friend, whom I greatly admire and respect and who had lost her marriage. I suppose the story of

Johnny Lingo continues to influence my subconscious because I thought, *She is definitely an eight-cow woman. She deserves an 8-cow man.*

Immediately I pictured the assessment of my friend as the title of a book—a book that would be original, fun to read, easy to understand, but inspirational enough to motivate the reader to action. I felt driven to write with these criteria. I elicited the help of anyone who could see my vision and wanted to help me conceptualize and write down my thoughts on Johnny, Sarita, and eight cows.

*On the island of Kiniwata, cows were symbols of wealth. My cows are symbols as well.*

On the island of Kiniwata, cows were symbols of wealth. My cows are symbols as well—representing something I believe is of far greater value in any relationship than mere financial status. My eight cows represent the character traits and values Johnny and Sarita each must have if they are to sustain a modern relationship. It is my observation that too many relationships are short of character. They are also often devoid of trust, respect, honesty, fidelity, and a litany of other virtues. They are sometimes built only on physical attraction and common interests. But that isn't enough these days. Actually it's never been enough.

Life and relationships are much more enjoyable when you have the requisite character traits—or cows, as I have chosen to call them.

I want this discussion to be fun and interesting but informative and useful as well. So, even though the nineteenth century is long gone, I recommend the following: In the spirit of Johnny Lingo and the traditions of Kiniwata: Sarita, you need to be an eight-cow woman; and, Johnny, you need to bring eight cows of your own to the table. Because, even now, *an eight-cow woman deserves an eight-cow man*."

# Got Cows?

*"Most people say that it is the intellect which
makes a great scientist. They are wrong: it is character."*
—Albert Einstein

*I* know the popular question is, "Got Milk?" but I figure the more fundamental query is, "Got Cows?" This may not seem to be a sensible question but regardless, that is what I am suggesting that we ask ourselves. Before I explain further, however, I would like to visit once again the beautiful island of Kiniwata, the home of Johnny Lingo, Sarita, and their eight-cow story.

I mentioned earlier that I often fantasized about the island of Kiniwata when I was young. And even though I have never found the island of Kiniwata on any map, I have longed to visit this island paradise to see if I could find anyone who descended from Johnny and Sarita. And, by the way, what happened to Johnny and Sarita? Did they grow old together? Did they stay happily married to the end? Was Sarita always Johnny's eight-cow woman? How could I find out the answers to these questions?

Well, that is the problem with fiction. Kiniwata isn't a real island, and Johnny and Sarita are just imaginary characters in a great story. But I still want to know what became of them! I guess I am a lot like those people who stay up at night after watching *Gone with the Wind,* wondering what really happened to Scarlet and Rhett. Some people might think, *Frankly, my dear, I don't give a . . .* But I really

*And, by the way, what happened to Johnny and Sarita? Was Sarita always Johnny's eight-cow woman?*

do care about things such as that. I particularly like to spend time contemplating what motivates each character. I also try to continue with the line of thought that created the story in the first place. By the time I finished scrutinizing the story of Mr. and Mrs. Lingo and their cows, Johnny and Sarita had all but transformed themselves from fictional characters into completely believable historical figures. That is why, regardless of the fact that everyone tends to comment on the obvious themes of respect and self-worth in the story of Johnny Lingo, I have extrapolated additional and perhaps more obscure points from the narrative.

First, I see Sarita, despite how she was treated by her father and others, as already being an eight-cow woman. That is one of the reasons why Johnny wants her. I don't see him bargaining for a two-cow woman in the hope of transforming her into an eight-cow woman. He already knows what she is worth.

The other not so obvious point of the story most people miss is that before Johnny could submit his unheard of offering for Sarita, he had to have eight cows! He didn't make a bold but empty promise. He paid eight cows—his own cows. The story makes it very clear—before Johnny could have his eight-cow woman, he had to be an eight-cow man.

*Johnny didn't make a bold but empty promise. He paid eight cows—his own cows.*

I remember when I first started thinking about these less evident parts of the story. I was listening to a discussion in Sunday School about "plain-Jane" Sarita and how Johnny had magically transformed her into this raving beauty. I wasn't buying their interpretation at all. Instinctively, I felt Sarita must have always been beautiful; Johnny just helped her to see it. Eventually, though, my mind drifted away from the conversation, and I thought, *Where do I get an eight-cow man? I want a man like Johnny Lingo!* Everyone was paying attention to poor Sarita while all I could see was Johnny. As I thought along these lines, it became clear why Johnny was so appealing.

Johnny's charm is that he was a man of action. To me, not one part of this story works if Johnny doesn't have his own eight cows. All of the romance would be lost if Johnny were to say in the bargaining process, "Look, Sam, I think your daughter is worth eight cows, but two cows are all I got." Sarita then becomes just another eight-cow woman arranged for on the cheap. No matter how Johnny feels about her value, she has been designated by his actions as a two-cow woman. He could whisper eight-cow nothings into her ear for the rest of her life, and all she would hear is, "You're only worth two cows." In the words, actually lyrics, of another famous fictional character, Eliza Doolittle in *My Fair Lady:*

> *Sing me no song! Read me no rhyme!*
> *Don't waste my time, Show me!*
> *Don't talk of June, Don't talk of fall!*
> *Don't talk at all! Show me!**

Yes! The magic of this story for me is a character whose actions spoke louder than his words. In fact, nothing in this story recounts anything that Johnny ever said to Sarita. He just stepped up to the bargaining table, paid his eight cows, and then went home and treated Sarita as the eight-cow woman she already was. It's a cinch to see Johnny wasn't a politician. No hollow campaign promises here. You see there is no guarantee of future cows. You either "Got Cows" or you don't "Got Cows."

To sum up, my take on the most relevant points in this tale are

*Lyrics by Alan Jay Lerner

19

that: 1.) Johnny took the time and effort to acquire eight cows of his own and 2.) Sarita through her goodness, humility, hard work, and despite the fact many people couldn't see it, was worth every one of them. All other lessons from the story just don't seem as important to me.

*There is no guarantee of future cows. You either "Got Cows" or you don't "Got Cows."*

Okay, I will admit it. I have really gotten caught up in the Johnny Lingo story. The problem of course is this is not the nineteenth century nor is it the island of Kiniwata. And the tradition of bartering for a wife is not a common practice in most parts of the modern world. I am sure some people would even view such a practice as somewhat primitive and barbaric. But before you become too critical I would like to point out that at least the people of Kiniwata had certain standards for courtship. And in light of the evolution of relationships in today's society, standards may be the one thing we lack.

In fact what are our standards? A friend of mine asked his daughter what attracted her most to the current "love of her life" and she stated, "I dunno. He's cool, I guess." My friend said he was hoping that a potential son-in-law would have a longer resume than just being cool. I discussed with him at length the concept of bringing specific cows to a relationship. He talked it over with his daughter and they laughed together when she said that despite the fact that she thought her boyfriend was cool, his lack of cows took some of the coolness away. Having the standard of eight critical cows was a new perspective for her and changed the way she looked at him for a long-term relationship.

I started talking to a few friends about bringing sufficient "cows" into a relationship. Not only did it make talking about their loved ones a little easier, it made it feel more constructive and a lot more fun. They even began making suggestions for what the eight essential cows would be. The idea was infectious. One person commented, "I wish my boyfriend would fatten up his cash cow!" Everyone burst out laughing—not because the topic wasn't serious but by discussing it in such a benign context the situation seemed repairable just by feeding the appropriate cow.

*Having the standard of eight critical cows was a new perspective for her and changed the way she looked at him for a long-term relationship.*

Of course it always helps when everyone in the discussion is familiar with the story of Johnny and Sarita. People such as I, who grew up with the story, got the gist of what we were saying from the title alone. My main point, however, that modern cows could represent character traits, usually takes a minute or two for anyone to completely appreciate.

In light of all the discussion and input I was receiving I decided I had better start keeping track of what people thought. So I created a simple survey. My original intent was to gather important data that could be analyzed by professional relationship therapists for years to come. But in reality my little questionnaire wasn't very formal or scientific. The survey basically told the story of Johnny and Sarita and then explained the concept of modern cows representing character traits. It then asked straight out, "What eight cows would you like to see in your relationship partner?"

In the end I only surveyed a few hundred people, but it felt like thousands because everyone I spoke to wanted to argue why their choice of cows was the way it really should be. Collecting and interpreting surveys, it turns out, can take a lot of time. Needless to say I was still surprised at the results. Johnny and Sarita, it seems, want exactly the same things—sort of. The difference usually involved approaching the same cow from different angles. But they still translated into basically the same eight cows.

It may be important also to point out here that it was determined that four cows from Johnny plus four cows from Sarita don't equal eight cows. The nature of the eight cows is such that it is vital for both Johnny and Sarita to have eight corresponding cows if they are to have a mutually satisfying relationship.

Take for example the Trusted Friend Cow. If only one person has that cow then there can't be real trust in the relationship. And if a person who has the Financially Responsible Cow is tied down with someone who doesn't have the same, then the frustration level could be catastrophic. The ideal in any relationship is to create symbiosis. When two people each bring all eight cows into the union, the combination has the greatest potential for happiness.

*The ideal in any relationship is to create symbiosis.*

Even though it is never too late to work on self-improvement and gathering cows, a marriage or a serious relationship isn't the ideal time or place to do so. Cow shortages have a tendency to turn a marriage into a balancing act between who has cows and who doesn't. This is why I encourage people to bring all eight cows to a relationship right up front. In fact, you should start gathering your cows before you even think about a relationship.

It is having the same foresight as the engineers who built train tracks to go over the Alps before there was a train even invented with enough power to actually make the journey. When the engine was finally built with enough horsepower to make the ascent, the tracks were already there. And, likewise, when you meet that special someone who makes your heart sing, trust me, you don't want to have to wait to gather your last two cows.

So . . . what are the eight cows? The next eight chapters will introduce the cows I derived from my surveys. I acknowledge that some of my cows are composites of character traits that just seemed to go well together. But all in all I have tried to remain true to the input I received. And even though there is plenty of room for debate, I feel they comprise eight critical cows or character traits necessary for a sustainable relationship. They are:

*Confidant Cow* or The Trusted Friend Cow
*Fire Cow* or The Passion for Life Cow
*Clever Cow* or The Wise and Witty Cow
*Cash Cow* or The Financially Responsible Cow
*Holy Cow* or The Spiritual Cow
*Wow Cow* or The Extraordinary Cow
*Cuddle Cow* or The Romance and Intimacy Cow
And *Considerate Cow* with multiple secondary names

We also identified an unwanted cow prevalent in far too many herds. It is called *Mad Cow.*

Most people I surveyed believe that having each of these cows, except for the *Mad Cow* of course, could help lead to a happier, more successful life—not necessarily an easy life, but a life that could overcome challenges and make a long-term meaningful relationship an achievable goal.

So, once again, "Got Cows?"

---

**Author's Note:** I mentioned earlier that I like to speculate on additional events not spelled out in an original story. Consequently each "Cow Chapter" begins with a Johnny and Sarita vignette I have written to set the stage for each cow presented.

# QUOTES ON CHARACTER

*"We aim to develop physique, mentality, and character in our students; but because the first two are menaces without the third, the greatest of these is character."*
— JOSEPH DANA ALLEN, HEADMASTER POLY PREP MAGAZINE

*"Character—the willingness to accept responsibility for one's own life—is the source from which self respect springs."*
—JOAN DIDION

*"If we want our children to possess the traits of character we most admire, we need to teach them what those traits are and why they deserve both admiration and allegiance. Children must learn to identify the forms and content of those traits."*
— WILLIAM J. BENNETT

*"Character is who you are and what you do when you think no one is watching."*
—ANONYMOUS

*"Good character is more to be praised than outstanding talent. Most talents are to some extent a gift. Good character, by contrast, is not given to us. We have to build it piece by piece by thought, choice, courage and determination."*
—JOHN LUTHER

# Confidant Cow

## THE TRUSTED FRIEND COW

*"Soul mates are people who bring out the best in you.*
*They are not perfect but are always perfect for you."*
—*Author Unknown*

*W*hen Johnny and Sarita were small children on the island of Kiniwata, they would often play together, catch fish, or gather tropical fruits and goodies to take home to their families. They enjoyed the time together. They were similar to most children—there was a lot of joking around and plenty of fun.

As they got older they continued to spend time together, but they would spend more and more time talking about the future and what they wanted out of life. One summer Johnny told Sarita of his plan to start trading with all of the other islands to build his fortune. To realize his dream, he would need to construct a large sturdy boat. Sarita had many responsibilities at home but would take every opportunity she had to help her friend build his boat.

When the boat was completed, Johnny and Sarita examined their work with satisfaction and a sense of accomplishment. The boat represented not only the beginning of a new life but was also an icon of their friendship and what they had shared over the years. As Johnny sailed away from the island embarking on his journey, he realized he was already counting the days until he could come back and be with his friend again. Sarita stared at the horizon until Johnny disappeared. They knew they would be friends forever.

*Friendship is a contract of the heart.*

*"She's just a friend"*—a simple phrase. It is routinely used as a flippant explanation for a relationship that doesn't have a lot of depth. It is too bad modern society often trivializes this important association. It used to be that a friendship was something worth fighting and dying for. A friendship meant everything. In reality, it still does.

During the Cold War, a man from Czechoslovakia was asked whether he considered the neighboring Soviets as brothers or friends. He answered without hesitation, "Oh, they are definitely our brothers. We can choose our friends."

So it is with life's many relationships—parent and child, husband and wife, partners in business, boss and employee, and the list goes on. All of these associations have something holding them together. Families are bound by blood. Husbands and wives are united by vows. Business partners work together by contract, and employees by virtue of a paycheck from their employer. But a friendship has no such arrangement. It is freely given and received. It has no written rules. Nor is it bound by any earthly document. Friendship is a contract of the heart.

A friendship can't be coerced or bargained for. It doesn't come as a right or privilege. It is a mutual meeting of hearts and minds—an unspoken bond of love, honesty, and trust. To those who truly understand its value, it is one of life's greatest possessions. But then, it really isn't a possession at all. It is more like a stewardship. Friends entrust each other with their very souls.

*Friends entrust each other with their very souls.*

Two character traits that both men and women prized highly in my survey were honesty and friendship. And in a close relationship, knowing your partner will always be a trusted friend really is one of life's greatest gifts.

28

The Trusted Friend Cow pretty much came in as a foundational cow—not necessarily as the most important to begin a serious relationship but labeled as the cow most likely to hold the relationship together. It is also called Confidant Cow because a confidant is someone you can trust above all others.

Throughout our lives we can acquire many different kinds of friendships. Some we call friends are just casual acquaintances, people we associate with during the day in varying degrees. Others we may like to socialize with; they are friends who are fun to have around. But a trusted friend is someone special. A trusted friend isn't just someone we like to party with or shoot the breeze with.

A trusted friend is a true confidant, a best friend, someone we share our lives with—the good, the bad, and the ugly. Such friends are nonjudgmental of each other. They are a valued part of each other's lives. Most people have very few such trusted friends. Some people have none. If you are in a close relationship, you should have at least one.

Johnny and Sarita should be trusting friends. Before deep romance and intimacy they need to be able to communicate and interact in all things as friends. Friendship will see them through the good times and the bad times. The loyalty they have to each other can soften any disagreement. The understanding between true friends overcomes all obstacles.

A memorable scene in the Civil War movie *Shenandoah* emphasizes the importance of friendship in a relationship. In the scene, a young lieutenant is asking Charlie (Jimmy Stewart) for his daughter's hand in marriage. The young soldier (Doug McClure) has just expressed his great love for her. I quote from the movie:

CHARLIE ANDERSON: *Do you like her?*

LT. SAM: *Well, I just said I . . .*

CHARLIE ANDERSON: *No, no. You just said you loved her. There's some difference between lovin' and likin.' When I married Jennie's mother, I-I didn't love her—I liked her . . . I liked her a lot. I liked Martha for at least three years after we were married and then one day it just dawned on me I loved her. I still do . . . still do. You see, Sam, when you love a woman without likin' her, the night can be long and cold, and contempt comes up with the sun.* \*

> I can't think of anything more heart wrenching than to be in love with someone you couldn't call a trusted friend.

Yikes! I can't think of anything more heart wrenching than to be in love with someone you couldn't call a trusted friend. I feel one of the greatest tragedies in a marriage is after years together and with the children gone, two total strangers try to make pleasant conversation across a lonely dinner table. When a real friendship doesn't exist, the golden years turn into desperate hours and days of dismal coexistence. But when you are in love and living with your best friend, every day can be filled with joy. When you

\*Written by James Lee Barrett

connect with your spouse as a lover and a friend, you can feel safe and comfortable just being yourself. In an effort to portray this feeling of security, Ralph Waldo Emerson wrote, "It is one of the blessings of old friends that you can afford to be stupid with them."

Bringing Confidant Cow into a close relationship is obviously very important. But just as every cow we will discuss, it needs to be regularly fed and cared for. True friendship can only flourish in an atmosphere of trust. George MacDonald, the great Scottish author and poet, wrote, "To be trusted is a greater compliment than to be loved."

What does it mean then, to be a trusted friend? I quote my friend Dr. Ty Erickson below:

> As a doctor, I know of the great responsibility that comes with being trusted. My patients entrust me with their very lives. Sarita and Johnny do the same with each other. When they both have this character trait, they can trust each other's motives and commitment to go the distance and not abandon the family. There will be a sense of security.

Trust is critical to the health and wellbeing of any relationship but most particularly in a marriage. Some may want to argue with George MacDonald's statement. Certainly, trust and love are both important, but love can only linger for so long when trust no longer exists. Conversely, love is able to grow and flourish when trust abounds.

Too many relationships and marriages have dark secrets introduced into them. A friendship can't flourish under such conditions. Secrets are a powerful herbicide that will eventually kill the flower of friendship. Friends expect each other to be forthcoming with all relevant information.

And while we are talking about secrets, trusted friends take each other into their most extreme confidence, often telling him or her things they have never before confided to another person. They expect their innermost feelings will be kept private, just between close friends.

> *Secrets are a powerful herbicide that will eventually kill the flower of friendship.*

Nonetheless, in a close friendship, trust goes way beyond just being honest or telling the truth. Friends *trust* that when they are down, their friend will lift them up. They *trust* that their friend will watch their back and stick up for them in public. They *trust* that their friend will also tactfully tell them when they have done something wrong or even if their hair is out of style. They *trust* that their friend will believe in them when everybody else casts doubts. They *trust* that their friend will be there to lend a hand when it is really needed and even when it isn't. Friends *trust* each other to share the good times and the bad.

A trusted friend is such a comfort in life, why wouldn't you want to be married to one? And more importantly, why wouldn't you want to be one as well? The friendship of Johnny and Sarita makes everything else in life a lot more enjoyable. And the trust they share makes it so much easier to delight in the other cows of the herd. The Trusted Friend Cow or Confidant Cow is my first cow because that is the very cow every good relationship is eventually built on.

Based on everything in this chapter, I hope you have an idea on how to be a trusted friend. But how do you recognize this cow in someone else? How do you learn to trust?

These are some pretty good questions. The answers don't necessarily come easily but they are available. It does require, however, the pretty old-fashioned idea of actually talking to each other. This leads us to a very important feature of every cow chapter. It is called *Conversations between Johnny and Sarita*.

*Conversations between Johnny and Sarita* contains statements and questions that couples can discuss openly and frankly with each other. These conversations are often very probing. It is amazing how much you can learn about another person when you have very clear-cut conversations about important topics rather than random comments about dinner or the movie.

It can often take some time to learn what makes another person really tick. It can be especially difficult when we want so much for that person to be as wonderful on the inside as they appear to be on the outside. Straight talk can speed up the process of discovery about another person. Don't wait to have the hard conversations until it is too late.

For example, I was once discussing with a couple which cows they thought should be included in the eight cows. The woman commented that her man would definitely need to have the Patience Cow. He immediately retorted, "Why? Are you going to try my patience?"

She thought for a moment and then said, "Yes. I can be very difficult at times. My man will have to be patient."

"Well, I am glad to know that up front," he sighed.

## Conversations between Johnny and Sarita.
### (Each bullet point is a conversation topic.)

- How important to you is a trusted friendship in our relationship?
- Do you consider me a trusted friend?
- Do you ever find it difficult to tell me the truth? When?
- If I have violated your trust, what can I do to rebuild that trust?
- Have you ever violated my trust? Do you trust me enough to share that incident with me?
- Do you think it is possible to truly trust another person?

# QUOTES ON FRIENDSHIP

———•◦•———

*"Lust is easy. Love is hard. Like is most important."*
—CARL REINER

*"Grief can take care of itself, but to get the full value of joy you must have somebody to divide it with."*
—MARK TWAIN

*"Oh, the comfort—the inexpressible comfort of feeling safe with a person—having neither to weigh thoughts nor measure words, but pouring them all right out, just as they are, chaff and grain together; certain that a faithful hand will take and sift them, keep what is worth keeping, and then with the breath of kindness blow the rest away."*
—DINAH CRAIK

*"Trust is the glue of life. It's the most essential ingredient in effective communication. It's the foundational principle that holds all relationships."*
— STEPHEN R. COVEY

*"The glory of friendship is not the outstretched hand, nor the kindly smile, nor the joy of companionship; it is the spiritual inspiration that comes to one when you discover that someone else believes in you and is willing to trust you with a friendship."*
—RALPH WALDO EMERSON

# Fire Cow

## THE PASSION FOR LIFE COW

*"The most powerful weapon on earth is
the human soul on fire."*

—*Field Marshal Ferdinand Foch*

$S$henkin was not a native of the islands. He had come with a merchant ship many years before and saw an opportunity to set up a modest import/export business. The climate suited him as well, so he decided to stay. He watched as over the years Johnny Lingo became more and more skilled at trading and anticipating the needs and wants of the people on the island. He knew Johnny was becoming very rich.

Shenkin noticed Johnny was most interested in the regular shipments he received from a specific English company. He seemed to prize these shipments above all others. He wondered what kind of riches these packages contained. Johnny always placed these orders in a sealed envelope and paid for them in cash. The shipments came consistently throughout the years.

Shenkin was a very scrupulous businessman. If his best client didn't want to tell him the content of these packages, he wasn't going to ask. But one day his curiosity got the best of him. It had been many years since he had visited Johnny and Sarita on the island of Nurabandi. Maybe he could pay them a visit and discover what this treasure could be.

When Shenkin arrived at Johnny's home he was amazed at how large and comfortably furnished it was. There were items from all over the world. Some parts of the home even had the new metal roof as well as a modern door and brick walls to protect it from the wind and rain. That must be where he keeps his greatest treasure, Shenkin thought.

Johnny and Sarita were more than willing to show Shenkin their lovely home. They ushered him through many fine rooms, each tastefully decorated with precious items they had collected over the years. They were all rare and magnificent. But it appeared they were saving the room with the modern door and brick walls until the end of the tour. Finally Johnny took a key from around his neck and inserted it into the handle of the door.

"Here is where Sarita and I keep our most valued possessions. These are the items we treasure above all others we have shown you. They represent Sarita's lifelong passion and it is now a passion I share as well. Our children also share this passion. And someday if we were to ever leave this island, the contents of this room would be the first items we would take. As the door swung open Shenkin peeked into the room.

To his surprise he saw rows and rows of beautiful antique shelves—full of books. Books of every kind. Picture books, novels, encyclopedias, maps, newspapers, and magazines. A full library here on Nurabandi!

"This is our passion, our greatest possession, and one we share with any villager who wants to participate with us. It will allow our children and our neighbors' children to be citizens of the world," Johnny stated.

As Shenkin headed back to the ship that would take him back to Kiniwata, he shook his head in amazement. He had always known the shrewd trader Johnny and his lovely wife, Sarita, were extraordinary people. But when he saw the passion Johnny and Sarita had for learning about the world through books and then sharing it all with the people of Nurabandi, he saw that they were even more extraordinary than he thought.

———•◆•———

Passion. Purpose. Dreams. Drive. Ambition. Fire! Almost every success book ever written talks about the importance of living each day with passion—having passion for life. The Fire Cow isn't merely the spark in a fabulous relationship, it is the roaring fire. Passion for life is the drive to live beyond one's self—to lose one's self in something bigger than ego. But the misnomer about passion is that it is an option. The reality is you either live your life with meaningful passion or that energy will be diverted elsewhere. The importance of the Fire Cow hinges on this very critical issue. I would like to clarify my point by referring to a classic tale.

*The Fire Cow isn't merely the spark in a fabulous relationship, it is the roaring fire.*

Most people have either read or heard of the book *Dr. Jekyll and Mr. Hyde,* by Robert Louis Stevenson. Many view it as a good premise for a monster movie. In fact, there have been more than a dozen renditions of this work—mostly B movies that continue to drive the important and timely message of this book into obscurity. One reader, however, who has examined the work more scrupulously, has called it,

"*. . . a fable that lies nearer to poetry than to ordinary prose fiction.*" —Vladimir Nabokov

Let's look closer at Mr. Stevenson's little gem. He wrote the story in less than three days while he was deathly ill of tuberculosis. Published in 1866, it was the manuscript that would give him his first taste of fame. Most of the serious analyses of his book quickly point out the seemingly obvious counterpoint of good vs. evil. However, deeper study shows a much more significant and disturbing message. It reveals how good men fall and why. This is how I see the story.

Dr. Jekyll was a respected man in the community. Everything he did was acceptable and honorable—but to him, boring. He was a prominent physician but no longer felt any joy in his life or his work—everything he did felt meaningless. He was raised to live a moral and ethical life. Dr. Jekyll was a man of principle without any passion for those principles. He was desolate inside.

*Dr. Jekyll was a man of principle without any passion for those principles. He was desolate inside.*

This emptiness drove Dr. Jekyll to seek for excitement and pleasure anyway he could. To find passion for something, he created an alter ego, Mr. Hyde. Mr. Hyde was full of life, exciting, and wild. But, unlike Dr. Jekyll, he had no values. He was raw emotion. As we learn in the story, this combination was disastrous. Mr. Hyde acted out his base desires without remorse. He was the embodiment of passion unbridled by principles.

Mr. Hyde proves to be Dr. Jekyll's undoing. Dr. Jekyll spends more and more time as Mr. Hyde. He becomes addicted to his own alter ego. He can't resist the feeling of aliveness when he becomes this hideous emotionally driven creature. Inside, Dr. Jekyll is mortified by the evil committed by Mr. Hyde but is continually drawn to him like a moth to the flame, until his untimely end.

Most see Mr. Hyde as the villain in this tale, but that is too obvious. The real culprit here is someone who knows right from wrong, has great prospects to do good, yet is unwilling to become passionate about his opportunities. Dr. Jekyll is the real monster here—and look around today, he can be seen everywhere, maybe even in the mirror!

Just as with Robert Louis Stevenson's book, most people like to point to the activities of Mr. Hyde above and label them as "the problem." But laziness, endless Internet surfing, excessive television, drugs, and addictions of all kinds are more symptoms than problems. They are the indicators of a life that has a dearth of spirit, of purpose, or commitment—the fire in such a person's life has been misdirected or numbed.

But let's not point fingers here, I use the term "Mr." for the sake of the story only. Both Johnny *and* Sarita are vulnerable to the insidious nature of a Mr. Hyde. But how do we keep the Dr. Jekyll side of our nature satisfied? How do we keep him from turning into Mr. Hyde? There is an old Native American fable that answers this question well:

As a Cherokee elder was teaching his grandchildren about life, he said to them, "A fight is going on inside me . . . it is a terrible fight between two wolves. One wolf represents fear, anger, envy, sorrow, regret, greed, arrogance, hatefulness, and lies. The other stands for joy, peace, love, hope, humility, kindness, friendship, generosity, faith, and truth. This same fight is going on inside of you, and inside every other person, too."

The children thought about it for a minute. Then one child asked his grandfather, "Which wolf will win?"

The Cherokee elder wisely replied, "The one you feed."

This well-known tale always ends there. I, however, would like to see the story extended with the question, "But, Grandfather, *what* do you feed it?"

For me, the answer to that question is passion! Passion is food to our soul. We must have it to live. Passion fuels and drives our efforts. The question posed by the story above is which side of our self are we going to feed our energy and passion to? In our first tale, our character at some point in his life stopped feeding any passion to his Dr. Jekyll persona, letting his Mr. Hyde side gorge himself on the excitement and energy previously reserved for the good doctor.

The Fire Cow is called the Passion for LIFE cow because LIFE is wholesome, worthwhile, and involves building people and creating goodness in the world. The opposite is death. It breeds destruction, selfishness, contempt, and a world full of hate. The Bible teaches there are only two choices—life or death. Which will you feed your passion to? Mr. Hyde led Dr. Jekyll to an untimely death and a similar choice will lead to the spiritual death of anyone who allows their Mr. Hyde to thrive in their life.

There is actually a science behind our need to express passion in our lives, for good or ill. It is not just left to the musings of storytellers and philosophers. When I first heard Dr. Ty Erickson's physiological explanation for our need for passion, a great deal of human behavior started to make sense to me.

People want to experience joy. Joy emanates from the natural hormones of dopamine and serotonin from the midbrain organ called the amygdala. As we enjoy our family, our relationships, our work, and our recreation our brains produce these important chemicals that bring joy. In fact the greatest stimulant of these natural chemicals comes through selfless service. Jesus proclaimed, he "who loses himself will find himself." As we lose ourselves in good work the passion that inspired the action works within us and literally our brain changes. Nitrous oxide is released causing the "good feeling" that attends good deeds. This is a short-lived molecule that if sustained through persistent virtuous living, will elevate the important neurotransmitters of serotonin and dopamine.

People who become depressed have low levels of these two chemicals and often will "self medicate." They employ a surrogate method of increasing these substances—succumbing to addictions. The use of alcohol, cocaine, tobacco, methamphetamines, and even pornography will raise the levels of these brain chemicals in an unnatural manner. Those who use these substances, will "feel passionate" for as long as the surrogate is in their system. But the stimulation will ultimately subside then collapse, and the addict will seek them again.

Passion is part of who we are. It is in each of us and is a gift from our Creator. God planted physical passions or appetites within each of us to help us thrive physically. Our appetite for food and water will help our bodies to survive and thrive. The physical attraction and passion between Johnny and Sarita lead to the creation of families. These passions or appetites are obvious.

*Passion separates man from the rest of earth's creatures. We seek to find and express a meaning in life.*

But not so obvious is the passion within us that feeds our spirit. This is the drive deep inside of us that seeks for fulfillment. This is the passion that separates man from the rest of earth's creatures. We seek to find and express a meaning in life. We naturally yearn to connect with our fellow man, with God, and leave a legacy. This is the passion that not only elevates us as individuals; it lifts all of humanity.

We are born with passions and appetites that are inherent in our natures and souls. They are not an option. But how you deal with them is. The wise Cherokee elder stated that the wolf you feed will win. Either you will choose good or evil, life or death, Dr. Jekyll or Mr. Hyde. Our passions and appetites will feed one wolf or the other. But why would anyone want to feed the wrong wolf? The key word here is WANT. What do you really want? If you don't know what you want, you won't know which wolf to feed.

*What do you really want? If you don't know what you want, you won't know which wolf to feed.*

I once knew a man who had the "perfect" family. He was married to a lovely woman. He went to church each week. Everything in his life looked great—except he wasn't happy, he had no passion for his life. He stated that everything he had done in his life was to fulfill the expectations of others—his parents, his religion, society, and his family. He didn't know what *he* really wanted. Over the next two years as a consequence of his lack of passion for his great life, he had an affair and ended up losing his wife, the respect of his family, and his membership in his church. Even his employment suffered.

Only after he had lost most of his previously unappreciated life did he finally become passionate about something—his old life! He wanted it back as he wanted air. He was on fire for the first time about things that were finally important to him. And unlike most stories like this, he won back his wife, his family, his church membership, and even his work thrived. He got back what he had lost. But his family finally got something they never had—they got him. Because this time they had his heart, his passion!

## So what do you want?

You can't let your parents, your church, society, or your friends decide that for you. You can only become passionate about what YOU want. Nobody is going to do this for you. However, be careful before you start pursuing your first impulses. Be sure to look ahead to see if what you want today will lead you to what you will want tomorrow. The present is connected inseparably with the future. If you want and get a life of self-indulgence and gluttony today you cannot escape a life of poor health and misery down the road.

*You can only become passionate about what YOU want.*

Dig deep. Look at the whole picture. Look at the present and the future. Connect with your Maker. Think about the real purpose of your life. Think about your talents, your gifts. Then decide WHAT YOU WANT. Find out what that is and pursue it with all the passion of your soul.

The Fire Cow was listed as very important by most of those I surveyed, but more particularly by those who were in relationships over five years old. Over time, it seems, the lack of a Fire Cow will cool off a relationship. The fire literally goes out. But the pain can linger for years, mainly because of the huge "if only" factor involved.

I have a friend whose daughter has had multiple relationships with "good" guys only to find they had no drive or ambition to accomplish anything in life beyond beating their last video game score. Eventually, each Dr. Jekyll she has been with has revealed his Mr. Hyde, and the relationship has ended.

Passion for your life is showing true gratitude to the One who gave it to you. Sharing those feelings in a loving relationship adds fire to the spark in both of you and gives you the ability to move mountains. Keep that fire burning, and your relationship can endure to the end of time.

## CONVERSATIONS BETWEEN JOHNNY AND SARITA

- What do you like to do most when nobody knows what you are doing? Is that your passion?
- If you could change the world, what would you change?
- If you could earn a living at anything you wanted, what would you do?
- Do you ever find yourself feeding the wrong wolf?
- Outside of our physical relationship, what passions do we share?

# QUOTES ON PASSION FOR LIFE

*"Passion, it lies in all of us, sleeping . . . waiting . . . and though unwanted . . . unbidden . . . it will stir . . . open its jaws and howl. It speaks to us . . . guides us . . . passion rules us all, and we obey. What other choice do we have? Passion is the source of our finest moments. The joy of love . . . and the ecstasy of grief. It hurts sometimes more than we can bear. If we could live without passion maybe we'd know some kind of peace . . . but we would be hollow . . . Empty rooms shuttered and dank. Without passion we'd be truly dead."*

—JOSS WHEDON

*"Your profession is not what brings home your paycheck. Your profession is what you were put on earth to do. With such passion and such intensity that it becomes spiritual in calling."*

— VIRGIL

*"If there is no passion in your life, then have you really lived? Find your passion, whatever it may be. Become it, and let it become you and you will find great things happen FOR you, TO you and BECAUSE of you."*

— T. ALAN ARMSTRONG

*"Nothing great in the world has been accomplished without passion."*

—GEORG WILHELM FRIEDRICH HEGEL

# Clever Cow

## THE WISE AND WITTY COW

*"Common sense and a sense of humor are the same thing, moving at different speeds. A sense of humor is just common sense, dancing."*
—William James

*T*he trading skills of Johnny Lingo were legendary in the islands. Many people thought he was just very lucky to always get the good deals when they came around. Young Hari, however, was curious enough to want to find out for himself how Johnny always fared so well in his trades. He became Johnny's little shadow. He watched as Johnny went to the open market in town. Other traders quickly examined the available merchandise and tried to make deals right away.

Hari noticed Johnny was much more relaxed. He would calmly

examine a couple of items here and there as if he weren't all that interested. He would eventually stroll over to the table with the most costly merchandise and begin to talk to the owner about something completely unrelated to his wares. He called the owner by name and asked him about his family. He then began to chat about his latest voyage to the big island. He told funny stories about the customs on the other side of the world, and the merchant roared with laughter. The other traders also gathered around to hear his tall tales and great adventures. Soon everyone was laughing.

Hari noticed, however, that while everyone was wiping away tears of laughter, Johnny would pick up the item he was most interested in. He offered the merchant a price lower than what he was asking and gratefully the merchant accepted. He was grateful because all of the buyers were now around his table, giving him the most opportunity to sell his items ahead of the competition.

Hari watched throughout the day. He saw that Johnny's wisdom and funny stories put everyone at ease. Every vendor was anxious to trade with Johnny, and Johnny was able to purchase everything he wanted at a favorable price. It was a good day. Hari was beginning to understand.

———— ◆ ————

Most people in my survey expressed interest in someone with a sense of humor. When pressed for details, however, the majority declared that what they meant by that request was not necessarily someone who could recall an endless number of mindless jokes but someone who could see the lighter side of the daily grind and laugh at the curves life can throw at us. The prospect of living with someone who is deadly serious all the time, it seems, can just take all the fun out of life. But then there are those who have a difficult time seeing it that way.

Let's look at one perspective.

*Personally, I don't get it. I believe that a sense of humor is overrated. Life is drop-dead serious. People are dying every day. There is tragedy and suffering throughout the world. The economy is in the tank and there is always a war going on somewhere—plus, I just got laid off and my children need braces. I don't think life is one bit funny and people who are laughing aren't paying attention.*

Wow! I'll bet this guy is fun to have around the house. But, is it possible to go to the other extreme—to try to find humor where it isn't? Let's look at another side of the coin.

*I once taught a Sunday School class of 16-year-olds. We were supposed to cover very important and sacred topics, but they would have none of it. Every minute of the class seemed to be filled with one-liners and light-minded comments. It was an all-out competition to see who could be the funniest. They all acted as though they were in a Sunday School sit-com—everything I was teaching seemed to be a set-up for the next joke. To them, humor was everything.*

Obviously there has to be a balance between Mr. Serious and our group of kids who thought everything should be funny.

The reality is that life is both serious and funny—happy and sad. There are tender moments and there are times of great excitement. There is a time for prayer and there is a time for dancing. The issue isn't necessarily a sense of "humor" as much as it is a "sense" of humor. Having this "sense" means you will see the lighter side of a flat tire and the seriousness of a friend's sorrow.

Having this sense is a balance between wit and wisdom. Benjamin Franklin, who was noted for his wit, was also known to be wise. His sense of perspective helped ease the tension among the delegates at the Constitutional Convention held in the sweltering hot Independence Hall in Philadelphia. In the vernacular of those days, such a person was considered "clever." Someone who has the Clever Cow is nice to have around. However, to many people I talked to, in light of the daily stresses of life and living, having this cow was deemed not just desirable but a necessity.

*The issue isn't necessarily a sense of "humor" as much as it is a "sense" of humor.*

No person wants to be around someone who treats every little problem as a major setback and ends up exploding in anger. A man who can make a good joke about a broken water pipe is telling his wife that everything is going to be fine. When a woman breaks her favorite piece of china, it is unfortunate. However, if she resists the temptation to get bent out of shape and take it out on her children, they will always know that they are more important to their mom than a pretty plate.

I am reminded of the sense of humor displayed by master cake artist, Duff Goldman. He claims that one of his culinary secret weapons is his ability to laugh at himself—A LOT! Before Duff became a well-known television personality he had entered a cake-decorating contest sponsored by the *Food Network*. His cake was very unique and very TALL. He and his brilliant crew had put their hearts and souls into the amazing creation. Everyone was oohing and aahing as he began putting on the finishing touches. Suddenly, the cake leaned a little and then came crashing down. The audience gasped—total disaster! In most contests of this intensity, a calamity such as this would bring either tears or anger—but not to Duff. Even as the cake was falling, his grin grew even wider, and when the cake hit the ground he let loose with such an infectious laugh that he became an instant star. The humor he finds, even in the disasters of his work, takes a lot of pressure off everyone and makes it a joy to be around him. Maybe that is how we should look at life.

*Even in extremely serious situations humor can be healing and therapeutic.*

Even in extremely serious situations humor can be healing and therapeutic. In the midst of the ravages of war, Bob Hope would use his unique brand of humor to entertain the troops—to lighten their day, perhaps their last day. Despite his numerous movies and TV appearances, this service he performed faithfully throughout his professional life will probably be his greatest legacy.

But even as you look on the lighter side, you still need to be able to appropriately deal with each situation. A man who laughs at the permanent-marker artwork of a 2-year-old on the kitchen wall may have a sense of humor. But the man who can laugh and then get the paint and fix it has a better sense of the situation.

If you have good sense, you will know when comedy is inappropriate. No mother wants to try to explain to a clown that Susie has a high fever and is having trouble breathing. At that point she is looking for a man, not a buffoon. Also, when humor is appropriate, you should laugh *with* your loved ones but under no circumstances laugh *at* them. An appropriate sense of humor will never make a person an object of ridicule. I will never forget the first time I heard an ethnic joke. I didn't "get it" at all. I still don't.

*You should laugh with your loved ones but under no circumstances laugh at them.*

It is nice these types of jokes are becoming less and less tolerated. But then any kind of humor that degrades or mocks another person shouldn't be acceptable, particularly in a relationship.

In my opinion, someone with a proper sense of humor will also never make light of the divine. Many, on the other hand, are anxious to create humor by mocking the sacred and embracing the profane. "It was offensive, but really funny," is a common justifying comment. Perhaps it was funny. But your perspective is out of whack when you are willing to sacrifice reverence for God and man for a laugh.

*Someone who is truly wise and witty recognizes that laughter is a gift from God—given to us to lighten our load, not to make light of the journey.*

A good sense of humor will keep life in perspective. It is sensitive to the nature of every situation. It has been said that a good funeral, like a good life, is full of both laughter and tears. The key is to know when to laugh and when to cry. Someone who is truly wise and witty recognizes that laughter is a gift from God—given to us to lighten our load, not to make light of the journey.

My friend Dr. Ty Erickson has a unique way of looking at a sense of humor:

> Someone who can laugh in the face of a stressful situation demonstrates a clear control of that part of the brain called the amygdala, the mid-brain from which emotion emanates. This part of the brain generates all of our emotions: happiness, sadness, anger, joy, and laughter. The

higher cortex modulates these feelings and places emotion in appropriate context. A pleasant sense of humor comes from the amygdala after the higher cortex has evaluated the situation and is able to recognize joy in the face of what seems to be a disaster.

This clinical analysis of humor may sound like just a bunch of scientific mumbo-jumbo, but what it really means is that such a person has control and discipline over his or her natural impulses. You can feel safe with such a person. You can laugh with them and never feel threatened. Johnny or Sarita can find joy even in the face of apparent sorrow.

*A Clever Cow not only sees the silver lining in the cloud but also finds a way to cash in on it.*

In addition to being wise and witty, to be "clever" is defined as being resourceful. A resourceful person can look at any situation from multiple perspectives. They will not only see the silver lining in the cloud but also find a way to cash in on it. Also, having the Clever Cow is a better stress reliever than any drug. The axiom, "Laughter is the best medicine," isn't just a section in the *Reader's Digest;* it's a fact!

I have a friend who was undergoing an emergency, life-threatening operation that required him to remain awake. Tensions were running high until at the most critical part of the procedure he cracked a completely unexpected and hilarious joke about the situation. Everyone in the operating room burst into laughter, and one of the doctors exclaimed, "He's going to live!"

When Johnny and Sarita have the Wise and Witty Cow in their relationship, come what may, they will be fine.

## CONVERSATIONS BETWEEN JOHNNY AND SARITA

- Do I take myself too seriously?
- Do I inappropriately laugh at the misfortune of others?
- Am I able to bring calm to difficult situations with my sense of humor?
- Am I ever too silly?
- Do I have a sense of perspective that allows me to be wise?

## QUOTES ON WIT AND WISDOM

*"A keen sense of humor helps us to overlook the unbecoming, understand the unconventional, tolerate the unpleasant, overcome the unexpected, and outlast the unbearable."*

—BILLY GRAHAM

*"A sense of humor is part of the art of leadership, of getting along with people, of getting things done."*

—DWIGHT D. EISENHOWER

# THE WIT AND WISDOM OF BENJAMIN FRANKLIN

—•◦•—

*"Three may keep a secret, if two of them are dead."*

*"Any fool can criticize, condemn and complain and most fools do."*

*"Either write something worth reading or do something worth writing."*

*"I guess I don't so much mind being old, as I mind being fat and old."*

*"Words may show a man's wit but actions his meaning."*

*"It is a grand mistake to think of being great without goodness and I pronounce it as certain that there was never a truly great man that was not at the same time truly virtuous."*

*"Be civil to all; sociable to many; familiar with few; friend to one; enemy to none."*

# Cash Cow

*"Money is only a tool. It will take you wherever you wish,*
*but it will not replace you as the driver."*

*—Ayn Rand*

$T$he story goes that early in his career Johnny had a fat Cash Cow. It was the envy of the islands. It gave lots of milk—rich in cream and full of flavor. It opened up opportunities for him to acquire many things and travel to other islands. When he would travel he would hire a "cow-hand" to take care of his beloved cow. He loved the freedom this gave him to stay away for extended periods of time.

However, after one lengthy trip, he came home to find that his Cash Cow was very ill and had stopped giving milk. What had happened? His Cash Cow had always been so reliable. He interrogated his hired hand at length to find the problem. But the boy only shrugged his shoulders and said that he was doing the best he could under the circumstances—what with the hay shortage and the contaminated grain that had been shipped to the island. The boy complained further by reminding Johnny that he was only being paid to milk the cow and feed it from the supplies provided by the feed store. "Oh, and by the way, I do need to be paid today," he reminded.

Johnny was in a panic. He had many bills due today. He was counting on the milk money to meet those obligations. But Johnny had fallen into a trap, the trap of relinquishing responsibility for his Cash Cow.

———•◆•———

Everybody it seems wants a Cash Cow. The term actually originated in the dairy industry. It described a cow that was paid for and would, year after year, give a steady, reliable supply of milk. The term was later applied to any division of a company that produced a consistent and dependable profit. These definitions of a Cash Cow are associated with responsible farmers or a company nourishing and taking care of a valued asset and then profiting from it.

Some people today, however, have a slightly skewed vision of what a Cash Cow might be. Many view their parents as their Cash

Cow, while others look to the government. Some look to get-rich-quick schemes while others erroneously view their good credit rating and debt as a Cash Cow. Some desperate folks look to winning the lottery or hitting the jackpot to provide their Cash Cow. These are not Cash Cows. A real Cash Cow denotes responsibility—financial responsibility.

*A real Cash Cow denotes responsibility—financial responsibility.*

It isn't possible nor is it my intention to teach a complete lesson on finances here. If, however, you want to learn all the principles of worldly finance, go to your local library or bookstore and pick up one or even several of thousands of books on the subject and knock yourself out. You can also attend lectures or listen to daily radio and TV shows on the subject. You can learn everything from personal finance to high finance or how to make a killing in real estate or on Wall Street. No matter which of the multiple money strategies you may choose, there are a few key elements a Cash Cow must have to work well for you personally and in a relationship.

I don't have any statistics to prove it, but based on what I have observed, financial issues appear to be one of the primary reasons why Johnny and Sarita divorce. However, it isn't money or the lack of money that seems to be the problem—how the money is managed is the real issue: who makes the money and how; how the money is spent and on what; how much is saved; how debt is managed; and how much debt is acceptable? These are the issues, and rational discussion and decisions on these points create the harmony or disharmony in Johnny and Sarita's home.

Ultimately, as in my story above, the most critical principle in caring for your Cash Cow is responsibility—you must take and maintain personal responsibility for your finances. And in a relationship the most important element that must be added to responsibility is communication. I would like to address each of these briefly and separately.

*To save our economy, our leaders have chosen to once again go to the Credit Cow for just one more fix—but will it be enough? Who knows?*

I am writing this book while our country and the world are going through an economic meltdown. Perhaps you find discussions on money and finances burdensome. But in the interest of Johnny and Sarita, stick with me. The present political climate is rife with finger pointing on all levels. Everyone is blaming someone else for our current situation. But ultimately, as the well-know axiom portrays, three fingers are pointing back at the accusers. There are only a precious few who have chosen responsibility over what was thought to be an endless line of credit. Foreclosures on family homes to closures of iconic American corporations are creating panic around the world.

To save our economy, our leaders have chosen to once again go to the Credit Cow for just one more fix—but will it be enough? Who knows? Despite your political views, the most important outcome I believe could emerge from our tattered economy is a lesson learned. That lesson is obviously to TAKE RESPONSIBILITY! NOW!

Being responsible for one's own Cash Cow falls first to Johnny and Sarita separately, and then when their Cash Cows are sharing the same pasture, they'll need to be responsible together. The best way I can think of discussing financial responsibility is by using the law of the harvest as the perfect template. But I want to make it simple. So here goes . . .

The law of the harvest involves: preparing the soil, planting the seeds, watering and cultivating, being patient, protecting, harvesting, and then storing.

To illustrate how this works in personal finances, consider these parallels:

- Preparing the soil—get educated, get smart, go to school, get trained, learn.
- Planting the seeds—go to work, launch your career, start your business.
- Watering and cultivating—work hard, work smart, excel and advance, grow your business or career, get smarter.
- Being patient—be patient.

- Protecting—get insurance, take care of your health, take care of your assets.
- Harvesting—get paid, collect your salary, realize a profit.
- Storing—save money, create equity, invest, avoid debt.

There you go—simple. It only gets complicated when you have to live it. The difficulty is having the discipline to apply the principles of each step without trying to take shortcuts, especially when there are so many shortcuts being offered. Take a shortcut at any time along the way and the yield of your crop is compromised. Shortcuts are only smoke and mirrors hiding the fact that the inevitable shortfall must be accounted for from next year's harvest and usually from many harvests to come.

*Shortcuts are only smoke and mirrors hiding the fact that the inevitable shortfall must be accounted for from next year's harvest and usually many harvests to come.*

One person I know who really understood and knew how to live the law of the harvest was my grandmother. Here is an experience I had with Grandma Helen when I was a young child, which illustrates why I say that.

One day I was watching Grandma apply her makeup. I noticed she was smearing something on her lips with a toothpick. When I asked her what she was doing she said that she was putting on her lipstick.

"That's not the way my mom does it," I exclaimed. "She doesn't use a toothpick, she just rubs it on."

My grandmother smiled and said, "I did that too until the lipstick wore down so far I couldn't do that any more. I'm using a toothpick to get the rest of the lipstick out of the tube."

"Well, most people just throw it away," I said.

Then Grandma said, "Let me tell you about the Great Depression . . ."

At the conclusion of Grandma's explanation, I had an "aha" moment that changed me for the rest of my life. And, yes, I still use a toothpick to get to the very last bit of my lipstick.

*Two people seldom have the exact same size or breed of Cash Cow.*

The opportunity to be "lipstick frugal" is all around us. We really don't have to wait for a depression or even a recession to apply the principle in our lives.

Taking personal responsibility for your individual Cash Cow is obviously very important. But two people seldom have the exact same size or breed of Cash Cow. As difficult as it is to successfully marry two people, marrying two Cash Cows together can be equally complicated. This is why communication in a relationship about finances, goals, and money in general is imperative. For Johnny and Sarita to become one, they must come to a consensus on financial issues before they can really feel united in all things.

Actually, before Johnny and Sarita even think about becoming a couple at all, they need to open the lines of communication on financial goals and procedures. The longer they wait to broach this topic, the harder it will be to come to a consensus on how they will handle money matters. Many wonderful people have completely different goals and financial skills. Despite their great attributes and plentiful cows, they should probably not continue the relationship until they resolve their financial differences. And I believe they are resolvable. Johnny and Sarita just need to come to a consensus before they open the joint checking account or joint anything for that matter.

*I have seen people make large, potentially crippling financial decisions without consulting their spouse. To most people, this is a type of betrayal.*

I have a friend who married the son of a very ambitious and successful businessman. She simply assumed her husband would be like his father. It wasn't until after they were married that she discovered his dream was to work his way up to be the manager at a local auto repair shop. But she wanted more. Neither was wrong. They were just wrong to not discuss it ahead of time. This lack of communication in their relationship, not just over financial issues, eventually led to their divorce.

Communication about finances need not necessarily be reduced to discussing every minute detail of household and personal expenses, but certainly on most decisions a consensus should be reached. I have seen people make large, potentially crippling financial decisions without consulting their spouse. To most people, this is a type of betrayal. Your companion can reasonably expect to be part of the decision process in these matters.

Additionally, couples need to communicate to one another their priorities. I think there is great wisdom in this quote by C.S. Lewis: "Put first things first and we get second things thrown in. Put second things first, and we lose both first and second things." When couples fail to prioritize, important matters can sometimes get neglected until a crisis occurs.

Probably the biggest contributor to stress and contention in finances is the Credit Cow. When you invite the Credit Cow into your herd, you are taking on risk and greater responsibility. You see, the Credit Cow doesn't belong to you, and its owner charges interest every minute it is in your pasture eating your food. And with this interest, the Credit Cow can be a virulent taskmaster. Consider this ominous description:

*The Credit Cow doesn't belong to you, and its owner charges interest every minute it is in your pasture eating your food.*

Interest never sleeps nor sickens nor dies; it never goes to the hospital; it works on Sundays and holidays;

it never takes a vacation; it never visits nor travels; it takes no pleasure; it is never laid off work nor discharged from employment; it never works on reduced hours. . . .

Once in debt, interest is your companion every minute of the day and night; you cannot shun it or slip away from it; you cannot dismiss it; it yields neither to entreaties, demands, or orders; and whenever you get in its way or cross its course or fail to meet its demands, it crushes you. —Author Unknown

Being very judicious with debt will help reduce stress over the years and, if they are patient, help both Johnny and Sarita realize their dreams over the long haul.

It is hard to say which of all eight cows is the most important. Each has merit. But of all the cows, I think the Cash Cow is one of the most important members of the herd because it helps to feed and provide for the other cows. Without the necessities of life, the other cows dwindle in importance. And it can be difficult to achieve your life's dreams without adequate funding. So, Johnny, Sarita, get your Cash Cow. Get it fat and keep it healthy.

## Conversations between Johnny and Sarita

- Do you feel I am financially responsible?
- Describe in detail the house, car, and lifestyle you expect to achieve in life.

- Do you consider yourself to be frugal or a spendthrift?
- Under what circumstances do you think debt is acceptable?
- Is there anything I do that sabotages our financial success?
- Do you consider yourself a hard worker?

## QUOTES ON FINANCIAL RESPONSIBILITY

*"You must take personal responsibility. You cannot change the circumstances, the seasons, or the wind, but you can change yourself."*

—JIM ROHN

*"Money is neither my god nor my devil. It is a form of energy that tends to make us more of who we already are, whether it's greedy or loving."*

— DAN MILLMAN

*"Don't ever underestimate the importance of money. I know it's often been said that money won't make you happy and this is undeniably true, but everything else being equal, it's a lovely thing to have around the house."*

— GROUCHO MARX

*"Annual income twenty pounds, annual expenditure nineteen six, result happiness. Annual income twenty pounds, annual expenditure twenty pound ought and six, result misery."*

—CHARLES DICKENS

# Holy Cow

## THE SPIRITUAL COW

*"Sometimes people get the mistaken notion that spirituality is a separate department of life, the penthouse of existence. But rightly understood, it is a vital awareness that pervades all realms of our being."*

—*David Steindl-Rast*

*O*ne day, Sarita's friend Moana was sitting in her hut reading the Bible. She enjoyed studying the teachings of what her mother called the "Book of books." She had a deep faith in God and tried to apply the words she read to her own life. But when her boyfriend, Tui, walked into the room and saw her reading, he began to make light of her activity. "You'll never catch me reading that stuff," he smirked. Moana sighed. She loved Tui in so many ways, but not being able to share her spiritual life with him was beginning to worry her about their future together.

Tui confided in his friend Johnny that Moana's "obsession" with religion was okay by him, but it just wasn't anything he was interested in. Johnny listened politely and then asked his friend, "How do you expect to grow together as a couple if you ignore, or worse, mock something that is so important to her? Do you really think that she will want to spend the rest of her life with that?"

"So you are taking her side, I see," Tui said, only half offended.

"Not at all," Johnny said. "I am not judging one way or the other. I know you have a spiritual side. I have seen it. And I know spirituality is important to Moana, but think about it, Tui—Why isn't it important to you?"

———·•·———

Sometimes called the Sacred Cow, the Spiritual Cow or Holy Cow was definitely listed very high by those who responded to my survey. But the concept of spirituality can be a little hard to package to every person's satisfaction. And the analogy of putting anything spiritual in a box may just describe the difficulty of defining this specific cow.

Even though my surveys showed a consensus on the importance of the Holy Cow, people were less definitive on exactly what that meant. Most, it seems, wouldn't be interested in having a close relationship with a Joan of Arc or St. Francis of Assisi—but some actually would. In defining spirituality, some include regular church attendance and adherence to specific religious codes of conduct and belief, while others want something less rigid yet perhaps more ethereal. Defining spirituality can be quite a task because it is often difficult to come up with a common reference point—it is a lot like trying to define "salty" without using the word "salt." And if someone has never experienced salt, how do you explain it to them?

*Becoming spiritual is a process similar to learning to crawl, then walk, and eventually run.*

Understanding spirituality and becoming spiritual is a process similar to learning to crawl, then walk, and eventually run. As with any process, the most important thing to do is BEGIN. Recently, one of the world's most brilliant philosophers and foremost atheists, Anthony Flew, proclaimed that the only rational explanation for the existence of the universe was a supreme creator. This conclusion didn't necessarily make him more spiritual, but it certainly makes for the most fundamental place to begin.

Even though our scientist friend above could reason that the wonders of the world and universe point to a creator, he never expanded that belief to an admission that there was a purpose to life. Maybe if he had lived longer, he might have reached that conclusion, I don't know. But most people see the existence of God our creator, the universe, and our earth home as a good indication that life has meaning. Furthermore, they see that connecting with God in some way can help us discover that meaning. Instinctively, most individuals feel that finding happiness in life depends on bringing their lives into some kind of harmony with their Creator.

Dr. Robert Fuller states:

> Spirituality exists wherever we struggle with the issue of how our lives fit into the greater cosmic scheme of things. This is true even when our questions never give way to specific answers or give rise to specific practices such as prayer or meditation. We encounter spiritual issues every time we wonder where the universe comes from, why we are here, or what happens when we die. We also become spiritual when we become moved by values such as beauty, love, or creativity that seem to reveal a meaning or power beyond our visible world. An idea or practice is "spiritual" when it reveals our personal desire to establish a felt-relationship with the deepest meanings or powers governing life.

Too often people measure their spirituality by checking off compliance to a list of rules and commandments. But spiritual leaders throughout the ages have taught that our relationship with the Divine is determined as much by our relationship with our fellow man as it is by obedience to a set of divine expectations.

Consider the following from Pujya Swami Chidanand Saraswatiji:

Spirituality is the essence of life. It is the light that shines on our lives, illuminating our paths, bringing light to the darkness, joy to the sorrow, and meaning to the incomprehensible. And the essence of spirituality? The essence of spirituality is service.

In my study of multiple religions, service to one's fellow man was considered a hallmark of spirituality—not just a piece of the puzzle but a full representation of ones' faith. Jesus said in the New Testament, *"Inasmuch as ye have done it unto the least of these my brethren, ye have done it unto me."* And *"He who says that he loves God and hates his neighbor is a liar."*

> *Service to one's fellow man is considered by many to be a hallmark of spirituality—not just a piece of the puzzle but a full representation of ones' faith.*

Is it any wonder that true spirituality would be such a desired cow? Johnny and Sarita are elevated above the mundane through constant service and devotion to each other when the Holy Cow is part of their daily life. Such service rendered to each other increases love and happiness. The relationship flourishes and life is perceived to have direction and purpose.

Another important attribute of the Holy Cow is gratitude. Being grateful for every gift that comes our way brings peace and contentment into our homes and happiness into our lives.

Dennis Waitley has said this about the relationship between happiness, spirituality, and gratitude.

> Happiness cannot be traveled to, owned, earned, worn, or consumed. Happiness is the spiritual experience of living every minute with love, grace, and gratitude.

Many of the finest things in life can be diminished by excess. Gratitude does *not* seem to be one of those. Few people have ever been accused of being "too grateful." It seems that the more gratitude we have the more we find to be grateful for. Consider the following from G. K. Chesterton:

*Many of the finest things in life can be diminished by excess. Gratitude does not seem to be one of those. Few people have ever been accused of being "too grateful."*

> You say grace before meals. All right. But I say grace before the concert and the opera, and grace before the play and pantomime, and grace before I open a book, and grace before sketching, painting, swimming, fencing, boxing, walking, playing, and dancing, and grace before I dip the pen in the ink.

The more gratitude we show in all things, the more we are able to draw closer to the Giver of the gift. Gratitude in all things brings us closer to God. Johannes A. Gaertner said it well:

To speak gratitude is courteous and pleasant, to enact gratitude is generous and noble, but to live gratitude is to touch heaven.

And Gordon B. Hinckley put this perspective on living a life full of gratitude:

Gratitude is of the very essence of worship. When you walk with gratitude you do not walk with arrogance and conceit and egotism, you walk with a spirit of thanksgiving that is becoming to you and will bless your life.

Real spirituality, in contrast to overt religious zealotry, is the essence of the Holy Cow. This does not mean, however, that religion and spirituality don't go hand in hand. They were never meant to be mutually exclusive. They should complement each other. Organized religion should create a community for support and service that enhances one's spirituality, giving it a broader opportunity for expression.

Some may ask why spirituality would be important in a relationship or why would one believe that the spirituality of their partner would be important. Part of that can be answered by Benjamin Franklin—one of the greatest writers of all time on the importance of having cows. (Of course, he referred to cows as character traits.) In this particular quote, Mr. Franklin clearly points out that our spirituality will affect the choices we make and to a large degree determine who we really are:

We stand at the crossroads, each minute, each hour, each day, making choices. We choose the thoughts we allow ourselves to think, the passions we allow ourselves to feel, and the actions we allow ourselves to perform. Each choice is made in the context of whatever value system we've selected to govern our lives. In selecting that value system, we are, in a very real way, making the most important choice we will ever make.

*Organized religion should create a community for support and service that enhances one's spirituality, giving it a broader opportunity for expression..*

Those who believe there is one God who made all things and who governs the world by his Providence will make many choices different from those who do not. Those who hold in reverence that being who gave them life and worship Him through adoration, prayer, and thanksgiving will make many choices different from those who do not. Those who believe that mankind are all of a family and that the most acceptable service of God is doing good to man will make many choices different from those who do not.

Franklin concludes:

Since the foundation of all happiness is thinking rightly, and since correct action is dependent on correct opinion, we cannot be too careful in choosing the value system we allow to govern our thoughts and actions.

An individual spiritual connection that governs our conduct is the foundation of the Holy Cow. Even though spirituality may be an individual matter it becomes a greater part of life when it is shared in a relationship. The Bible and other religious texts teach that a man is not to be without the woman and the woman should not be without a man. Obviously on the physical level a man and woman are two halves of a whole. But perhaps we should be equally aware of the synergy we can have as a couple when we unite spiritually.

Even though you may accomplish great things spiritually as an individual, in a meaningful relationship where you share the same religious perspectives you often are able to offer much more. When the great violinist Isaac Stern selflessly entertained the troops in every conflict from World War II to the 1991 Gulf War, it was often without accompaniment. No one would dare say his offerings weren't anything but wonderful. But as good as Mr. Stern was, he could not play all of the notes of most violin pieces by himself. It is only with full accompaniment that the music in all of its sublime majesty can be experienced.

So it is with us. We should be able to offer a proper accompaniment to the spiritual solo of our partner. In most aspects of a good synergistic relationship 1 + 1 = 3, but in spiritual matters 1 + 1 + God = well, who knows? Jesus taught that with God all things are possible. When each of you brings a Sacred Cow to your union it can make your relationship all that it should be and could become.

---

*Even though spirituality*
*may be an individual*
*matter it becomes a*
*greater part of life when it*
*is shared in a relationship.*

---

## CONVERSATIONS BETWEEN JOHNNY AND SARITA

- Do you believe in God?
- How do you feel when you think of Him?
- Does your belief play an active role in your life and decisions?
- Do you plan on teaching your children your beliefs?
- Do you think having similar beliefs is important in a close relationship?

## QUOTES ON SPIRITUALITY

*"It is the heart which experiences God, not the reason."*

— BLAISE PASCAL

*"A humble knowledge of oneself is a surer road to God than a deep searching of the sciences."*

—THOMAS A' KEMPIS

*"Deep down in every man, woman, and child, is the fundamental idea of God. It may be obscured by calamity, by pomp, by worship of other things, but in some form or other it is there. For faith in a Power greater than ourselves, and miraculous demonstrations of that power in human lives, are facts as old as man himself."*

— ALCOHOLICS ANONYMOUS

*"So I would hope they would develop some kind of habit that involves understanding that their life is so full they can afford to give in all kinds of ways to other people. I consider that to be baseline spirituality."*

—SUSAN SARANDON

*"All day I think about it, then at night I say it. Where did I come from, and what am I supposed to be doing? I have no idea. My soul is from elsewhere, I'm sure of that, and I intend to end up there."*

—JALAL AD-DIN RUMI (PERSIAN POET AND MYSTIC, 1207–1273)

# Wow Cow

## The Extraordinary Cow

*"You don't love someone for their looks, or their clothes, or for their fancy car, but because they sing a song only you can hear."*
—*Author Unknown*

When Johnny was setting up his business, he would often spend many months at a time away from home. He met lots of interesting people, including many very beautiful women. Some of them were very fond of Johnny and would invite him to lavish celebrations and luaus. He noticed that even though many of his new "friends" treated him very well, they would often treat others, such as the food servers or the hired help, very poorly. This bothered Johnny. He began to miss the simple island of Kiniwata.

He thought of Sarita. She also treated him very well. But she treated everybody kindly as well, even those who could offer her nothing in return. He remembered the time Sarita nursed an injured dog back to health. She was also kind to children. He remembered how thoughtful and helpful she was to her father, even though he was seldom grateful. She explained that she knew her father was sad after her mother had died and that he was only gruff and inconsiderate because of pain.

Johnny had many offers for relationships with the daughters of chiefs and other very important people, but the more he thought about it, the more he knew he would miss the charitable nature of his lovely Sarita. She was beautiful, yes. But her kindness made her even more beautiful—on the inside. To him, this is what made Sarita special above all other women. He couldn't wait to get home.

———•◆•———

One of the most exciting things I encountered while researching cows was the discovery of the Wow Cow. Probably like you, I had never even heard of a Wow Cow before. But as I began to question people about the character traits and qualities they were looking for in a companion, I noticed that many of the surveys contained a unique cow that seemed to be extremely important to that particular person.

At first I felt that these were just random cows reflecting the inherent differences of the people questioned. But on closer examination

I determined all of these cows were just different manifestations of the same cow—the Wow Cow. I discovered that the Wow Cow represents the one thing about you that makes you unique—special—extraordinary! But more importantly, it also may make you especially interesting to a select group of people, or maybe even only one person, who is attracted to your distinctive quality or qualities. When you come to the bargaining table with this cow, the right person could very likely say, "Wow!"

*Work to be the best YOU possible, and your Wow Cow will begin to stand out from the herd.*

So what is your Wow Cow? Well . . . what would you want it to be? Of course, as they say, the sky is the limit. But you can't just choose to be Michael Jordan or Kelly Clarkson. What you can do is what they did by developing and nurturing the talents and abilities God has given you. Work to be the best YOU possible, and your Wow Cow will begin to stand out from the herd. And it may surprise you when you begin to see what your Wow Cow is.

Perhaps you have the gift of making people feel good about themselves. Maybe you are intensely spiritual, extremely charismatic, or so good with money that you will be an exceptional provider. It could be that you are very loyal or incredibly fun to be around. You might be extraordinarily talented in one way or another or you may just be drop-dead gorgeous and a pleasure to look at! The list of possibilities is endless. This is your special cow. To use a common term, it is your ace in the hole.

There is no such thing as a generic person. Everyone is unique. Everyone has at least one Wow Cow. Some people have Wow Cows that are highly developed, fat, and healthy. Others aren't aware that they even have a Wow Cow. Some have several Wow Cows while others have a few, or only one. It is similar to Jesus' parable of the talents. And as that parable teaches, it is very important to develop and nurture your talents, abilities, and virtues.

*There is no such thing as a generic person. Everyone is unique. Everyone has at least one Wow Cow.*

Even though you may have many Wow Cows, a specific person will most likely single out only one they find to be especially attractive. Your Wow Cow is what causes that person to take a second look. If you have many Wow Cows, naturally you will attract a wider variety of people. This gives you more choices in finding someone who may interest you as well. And of course, it goes without saying that many will have no interest in your particular Wow Cow.

A person may very well be drawn to your Wow Cow because their goals in life may be similar to yours. Your unique talents and virtues will help them to feel that the both of you could be happy together pursuing the same ambitions and dreams. This places a big responsibility on you to keep your Wow Cow healthy and thriving.

Too many people fail to tend and nourish the very cow that created the mutual attraction in the first place. Worries and stresses of life often intrude and cause us to forget the importance of this cow. This of course is a very big mistake. When the Wow Cow is allowed to die or stray from the herd it may be perceived that the Wow Cow was not real and was merely used as a lure to encourage the relationship. When you neglect or fail to nurture the intriguing facets of your personality, it could take some of the wow out of a marriage, leading to feelings of resentment and regret. Couples should work together to keep their dreams alive. This shared vision will help keep them close and working together.

*Too many people fail to tend and nourish the very cow that created the mutual attraction in the first place.*

Not every talent or skill can really be considered a Wow Cow. Proficiency at video games shouldn't be deemed a Wow Cow. Neither should the ability to quote sport statistics ad nauseam be viewed as having any real lasting appeal. But then I'm not necessarily trying to be the judge of Wow Cows. The sport statistics Wow Cow may very well make its owner into an excellent sportscaster. The important point is to develop the best Wow Cow that you can.

Even though you may have a pretty terrific Wow Cow, it is important to remember that you must still bring at least seven more cows to the bargaining table. Wow Cows have such a significant attraction factor that many times people overlook the need for the other cows. It can be very disappointing when your Wow Cow is all that you bring to a relationship. A really great Wow Cow without the requisite other cows will likely lead to the failure of a relationship and subsequent broken hearts.

When you love someone whose Wow Cow makes your heart beat faster and stirs your soul, you project your life with this person and imagine the happiness and fulfillment you could have together. Because of the power of the Wow Cow you understand the potential for synergy and the endless possibilities resulting from the passions you share.

To illustrate this concept, imagine three couples boarding an airplane from San Francisco to Hong Kong. (It is a 16-hour flight.) One couple seems to disagree on everything. They are still fighting over things they should have packed and last week's argument over finances. As you watch this couple you wonder what they could possibly have in common. It looks as though it is going to be a very long, long, long, flight. The second couple seem indifferent to each other. They appear to be two strangers who just happen to be sitting next to each other. They are polite but don't seem to be actively engaged in each other's life. They hope to get some sleep on this boring ride. The third couple is alive with excitement. They are discussing past successes and future plans for projects they are working on together. They radiate enthusiasm and appear to welcome the flight ahead as a wonderful opportunity to spend time together. For them time will "fly."

At the end of the trip, all three couples deplane in Hong Kong. They have all spent sixteen hours in the air and have arrived at their destination. The first couple looks as if they have been pulled through a knothole. The trip really took its toll, and they are as contentious as ever. The second couple looks even more groggy and disengaged in each other than before. The third couple gets off the plane full of excitement. The time together allowed them to share their mutual passions. They made great plans. They can't wait to get started.

Such can be your life when you spend it with someone who enjoys and shares your Wow Cow. The trip is exciting and enjoyable and way too short. You are excited beyond words when you think about being with this person. There's a lot to be said about being equally yoked in a marriage, where each values the other's Wow Cow. When you understand the unlimited possibilities of two people sharing the power and joy of this relationship, you will know why it is so important to have the rest of your cows.

It is also important to point out here that even though your Wow Cow may be highly appreciated and loved, it does not necessarily have to be the same for both Johnny and Sarita to enjoy the exhilaration of this cow. You may be a gifted artist while your companion may still struggle with stick figures. What is important is that the less artistic spouse is capable of enjoying the other's art. His or her continued interest in their partner's Wow Cow will assure that their talent will have a place to grow and flourish. *Compatible Wow Cows are the issue.*

Compatible Wow Cows are similar to good music. A piano has 88 keys or notes. Unique combinations of notes create sounds that attract different listeners. Some people enjoy jazz, others classical, gospel, or pop. Every person's Wow Cow represents a note, a unique "sound." Two resonant notes come together to create harmony. Each note "seeks" the WOW of another note to create this beauty. We see the WOW in others as something we would enjoy resonating with. But certain notes don't blend well. They create a discord, an awful sound. These notes aren't individually bad they are just incompatible. If any and all notes combined could create great harmony, then you could probably play the piano with your fist. And if everyone sought the same Wow Cow it would be as boring as a piano with only one functioning key.

*If any and all notes combined could create great harmony, then you could probably play the piano with your fist.*

It is very important to keep the Wow in your Wow Cow. Your seven other cows will sustain your relationship in many important ways, but your Wow Cow adds an extra dimension of joy that provides zest and excitement. Having compatible Wow Cows can make it so you wake up every morning for the rest of your life and look at your mate and think, *Wow! I am so lucky.*

## Conversations between Johnny and Sarita

- What do you think your Wow Cow is?
- What do you think my Wow Cow is?
- Am I taking proper care of my Wow Cow?
- Do I have more than one Wow Cow?
- Do you think I sufficiently appreciate and support your Wow Cow?

## WOW COW QUOTES

*"Life is not a journey to the grave with intentions of arriving safely in a pretty well-preserved body, but rather to skid in broadside, thoroughly used up, totally worn out and loudly proclaiming . . . WOW! What a ride!"*

—Author Unknown

*"When you are inspired by some great purpose, some extraordinary project, all your thoughts break their bonds. Your mind transcends limitations, your consciousness expands in every direction, and you find yourself in a new, great, and wonderful world. Dormant forces, faculties and talents become alive, and you discover yourself to be a greater person by far than you ever dreamed yourself to be."*

—Patanjali

*"Our whole life is an attempt to discover when our spontaneity is whimsical, sentimental irresponsibility and when it is a valid expression of our deepest desires and values."*

— Helen Merrell Lynd

# Cuddle Cow

## THE ROMANCE AND INTIMACY COW

*"Romantic love reaches out in little ways, showing attention and admiration. Romantic love remembers what pleases . . . what excites . . . and what surprises . . . Its actions whisper: You are the most special person in my life."*
—Charles Stanley

*S*everal years after Johnny and Sarita married, Sarita was spending the afternoon with her friend Ulani. It was the middle of the afternoon when Johnny came home early from the village. He greeted Ulani and then asked politely if he could borrow Sarita for a moment. Ulani laughed and consented.

Johnny took Sarita in his arms and gave her a big kiss. He then stroked her hair and looked deeply into her eyes and asked if there was anything he could do for her since he was home early. She paused and then said she could use some water from the nearby river.

Ulani gasped quietly. "That is women's work!" she thought.

Johnny said gently and without hesitation, "I would love to, Sarita." He looked fondly for a long moment into Sarita's eyes once more and kissed her tenderly. He then grabbed the water jugs and bolted toward the river.

As Johnny left, Sarita sighed with contentment. Ulani stared in amazement and said, "Sarita. I always knew you were the luckiest girl on the island. But today I feel that you are the luckiest woman in the world."

Sarita just smiled and nodded her head in agreement.

———•◆•———

The Romance and Intimacy Cow or Cuddle Cow is a very special cow. It very well could be Sarita's favorite. It gives chocolate milk and eats only flowers—and even though all of the other cows are important, this is the cow that makes Johnny, Sarita's and Sarita, Johnny's—exclusively.

You see it isn't just about gathering cows—filling a grocery list of desired attributes. It is also about sweeping someone off their feet—making them feel special—making them feel truly loved and cherished. Your other cows may make you worthy to approach the bargaining table, but this is the cow that ultimately must be accepted before the relationship can really take off.

*When a person or a couple tries to skip romance and go straight to intimacy, they are missing the whole point.*

Some may think that the words *romance* and *intimacy* are synonyms, but I don't think they are. Yes, they both involve a relationship that should only be shared with one special person, but romance focuses on the emotional aspects of togetherness while intimacy mostly has to do with the physical closeness of a couple. They are, however, intended to go hand in hand—with romance leading the way. And when a person or a couple tries to skip romance and go straight to intimacy, they are missing the whole point.

I will try to explain . . .

True intimacy between a man and a woman begins in the heart—and romantic behavior is the manifestation of those feelings. The first indication of heart-felt affection may be a kind act, a compliment, an admiring look, or a word of encouragement. These small gestures speak volumes, and they set the stage for intimacy.

Romance is anything that stirs the heart to feelings of affection and longing. Romantic behavior is an admission of the attraction one feels toward another. Through romance we make ourselves a little vulnerable, for our tender feelings may not be reciprocated and we stand the chance of being rebuffed and humiliated. Still, the rewards of discovering that another shares the same feelings we have for them make it worth the risk. Practiced over a lifetime, romance serves to keep those original, heady, and exciting emotions alive. It can be as simple as a note in a lunch box, a hand with the dishes, an unexpected gift, a diaper voluntarily changed, or a hug in passing—each is a step in the waltz that leads to intimacy.

Spontaneous acts of kindness, being sensitive to each other's needs, generosity, and making time for each other will keep the music playing. Physical intimacy then becomes a wonderful celebration of all the tender moments preceding it.

Many people, however, have little concept of the principles discussed above. Many have sex first and then are disappointed when a meaningful relationship doesn't result from the physical pleasure. They have difficulty putting physical intimacy in its proper perspective because they focus on the act itself instead of the romance that should lead to it. It's similar to watching the celebration after a televised football game instead of watching or participating in the actual game. The celebration doesn't have any meaning if you haven't paid

> *Spontaneous acts of kindness, being sensitive to each other's needs, generosity, and making time for each other will keep the music playing.*

attention to the game—and without the game, why are you even celebrating?

Romance is a wonderful game that shouldn't be missed or neglected. And physical intimacy is a celebration—it is also the ultimate act of giving one's self to another. But in this area, Johnny and Sarita don't have the same needs or desires. In my chapter "Got Cows?" I mentioned that the men and women in my survey wanted the same things but often approached the same cow from different angles. This is one of those cows. Romance and intimacy is a vital component of any close relationship between Johnny and Sarita. But it is important to acknowledge the differences between men and women when discussing the subject. I would like to quote Dr. Mark Dowdle who specializes in relationship issues when he is not busy being a gynecologist.

Libido or sexual desire is a large component in the complex experience of intimate relationships. The response, however, is very different between men and women. Men tend to be more hormone-driven and interested in getting straight to the intimacy. Women, on the other hand, seem to have the need for what I call the seven T's for romance, they are: talk, time, touch, tenderness, timing, trust, and the last T being testosterone. Women, like men, require testosterone to initiate a drive toward intimacy. Women however have a significantly smaller amount of this hormone, making romance, or the six other T's, much more important to them on both an emotional and a physical level. Failure to recognize these differences can create frustration where there should be fulfillment.

Intimate relations ideally involve one man and one woman who are united by promises they have made to each other in front of God and several witness, usually con-sisting of friends and family. To me this is the most beautiful and meaningful relationship between a man and a woman. Intimacy within this bond can be one of life's greatest pleasures. Too often, though, Johnny's or Sarita's heads are turned away from each other to sen-sual activities that don't include their spouse.

*When romance wanes, intimacy can become just another obligation— a task to cross off our to do list.*

It seems harmless at first, just to look, but soon the heart and then the soul follow, and Johnny and Sarita are left wondering what happened to the magic in their marriage. They seem to be drifting apart. There is indiffer-ence and emptiness in the eyes—coldness in the heart. They assure each other it is just stress at work or the burden of family life. Thus the lying begins and the oneness is gone.

I have often wondered how someone would know their spouse was heading down forbidden paths and be able to stop them before the betrayal. To me, romance is the key. Romance is fuel for the fire of intimacy. When romance wanes, intimacy can become just another obligation—a task to cross off our *to do* list. And when romance is ignored, couples are much more easily lured by the siren song of infidelity, which almost always snuffs out whatever flame might have remained in their intimate relationship.

Johnny and Sarita! Don't underestimate the importance of romance in your relationship, especially after marriage. Romance keeps your love alive and will help keep the feelings and desire for intimacy as special as before.

Here is a list of some of my favorite acts of romance:

- Romance is my own pet name, meant for me and no one else.
- Romance is a foot rub without expecting one back.
- Romance is a love note in grease pencil on my mirror.
- Romance is finding my favorite candy under my pillow.
- Romance is our own date, just you and me, a table set for only two.
- Romance is seeing you stand on the porch waving good-bye until my taillights have faded.
- Romance is sitting next to me in church, holding my hand, with our children on either side of us.

- Romance is a midnight kiss on New Year's Eve and every night after that.

Dr. Ty Erickson adds:

We are biologically driven to find our mate. God placed in our bodies the instinct to procreate and have a family. The marriage vows bring the most beautiful expression of love. This union between Johnny and Sarita makes them of one heart. Ponder for a moment what it means to be of one heart. As humans we have two kidneys, two arms, two legs, two eyes, two ears even two halves of a brain. But we have only one heart. Within my specialty as an OB we occasionally will see conjoined twins—two little babies bound together with some shared organs. Often they can be separated—but not if they share the same heart. If we try to separate a shared heart, either or both the twins will die. Similarly when we have become one with our spouse, sharing the same heart, we beat in sync. We love to be together and we miss each other while away. We are spiritually conjoined.

Many who will read this book long for such a relationship—those who are now widows or widowers, separated, divorced, or never married. My heart yearns for you who have never had or who have been deprived of the kind of joyful relationship I have described. My plea to you, Johnny and Sarita, is that you will cherish and preserve what you have. Do all in your power not to break each other's hearts. Live for each other. Snuggle. Hug. Kiss. Caress. Serve. Give. The Cuddle Cow is so important that it might as well be called the Happiness Cow or Cow of Eternal Bliss. And it is more than chocolate and flowers. It really is a union of two souls and living exclusively for each other—becoming one!

## CONVERSATIONS BETWEEN JOHNNY AND SARITA

- Do you consider me to be romantic?
- What do you find romantic?
- How do you feel about "wandering eyes" in a relationship?
- What do the words tenderness and sensitivity mean to you?
- Do you think we make enough quality time for real intimacy?

# QUOTES ON ROMANCE AND INTIMACY

*"We are all born for love. It is the principle of existence, and its only end."*

—BENJAMIN DISRAELI

*"The married are those who have taken the terrible risk of intimacy and, having taken it, know life without intimacy to be impossible."*

—CAROLYN HEILBRUN

*"Love itself is what is left over when being in love has burned away, and this is both an art and a fortunate accident. Your mother and I had it, we had roots that grew towards each other underground, and when all the pretty blossom had fallen from our branches we found that we were one tree and not two."*

—ST. AUGUSTINE

*"What greater thing is there for two human souls than to feel that they are joined together to strengthen each other in all labour, to minister to each other in all sorrow, to share with each other in all gladness, to be one with each other in the silent unspoken memories?"*

—GEORGE ELIOT

*"True love does not come by finding the perfect person, but by learning to see an imperfect person perfectly."*

—JASON JORDAN

# Considerate Cow

*"Your greatness is measured by your kindness; your education and intellect by your modesty; your ignorance is betrayed by your suspicions and prejudices, and your real caliber is measured by the consideration you have for others."*

—Olin Miller

When Johnny and Sarita were young they had many responsibilities at home with their families. Johnny's father was a fisherman. He also cultivated some land and raised several animals to sell at the market. When his father was away at work, it was Johnny's job to tend the animals and weed the garden. It was also very important that the cows and goats be milked on time.

But Johnny was a dreamer. He would often take time off in the middle of the day to go to his favorite lookout point over the ocean and gaze out to sea, planning his future. One day Sarita walked past Johnny's home and noticed the cows and goats were in desperate need of milking. Johnny was nowhere to be found. Knowing the trouble Johnny would be facing if his father came home to the situation, Sarita slipped under the fence and spent the next two hours finishing Johnny's chores.

Johnny woke up in a panic. He had fallen asleep atop his lookout point. The sun had slipped below the horizon and it was quickly getting dark. He knew he was in deep trouble. His father was going to be so angry! As Johnny raced into the yard, his father was standing there to greet him.

"Johnny. You have made me very proud! Not only did you do your chores well, but you also cleaned out the animal pen and straightened up the storage shed. Thank you."

Johnny was stunned.

The next day when he met Sarita he questioned her about her considerate act. She just shrugged and said, "It's okay. You would have done the same for me."

———•◆•———

The great American architect Frank Lloyd Wright once said, "God is in the details." In the relationship between Johnny and Sarita it could also be said, "Joy is in the little things." Daily thoughtfulness, kindness, and consideration between Johnny and

Sarita make the rough roads smooth, the choppy seas calm, and the difficult times . . . well, seem less difficult.

The Considerate Cow is all about putting the needs and wants of others in a position of significant priority. John F. Kennedy well defined the concept of being considerate when he stated, "Ask not what your country can do for you. Ask what you can do for your country." Even though his statement wasn't meant to apply to every level of society, perhaps it should—and nowhere more fundamentally than in a relationship. The opportunity to show daily acts of selfless consideration can bring the greatest long-term joy to both Johnny and Sarita.

*The Considerate Cow is all about putting the needs and wants of others in a position of significant priority.*

On the surface, the Considerate Cow appears to be the embodiment of the Golden Rule. When you have this cow you treat others as you would like to be treated yourself. You create in your home a sense of equity and fairness. When both Johnny and Sarita live this principle, there can be a balance—equal give and take. But then, most people know that relationships seldom achieve this balance. The way your companion wants to be treated may not be the same as you. That is why in a relationship, one might consider the higher standard of the Platinum Rule.

The Platinum Rule states that one should try to treat others as they would *want* to be treated. This puts a responsibility on you to determine what the other person really wants. No longer can you passively do unto others according to how you see it. You really need to connect with that person and be considerate of *their* innermost thoughts and desires in order to most effectively "do unto" them.

Being considerate is an act of love. Jesus taught of a loving God. He also said that one of God's attributes was that he knows our needs before we ask. I believe the more we love someone the easier it is to know what they want and need. And the more consideration we show through selfless acts of kindness the more we will love that person.

At first, I couldn't think of a good story or an example from history to illustrate being considerate. Examples of selfless service tend to be small, unsung acts performed behind the scenes. Then I thought of all the acts of heroism performed daily on the battlefields of war and life. All of us admire those who out

*The way your companion wants to be treated may not be the same as you. That is why in a relationship, one might consider the higher standard of the Platinum Rule.*

of love, loyalty, or duty sacrifice their own lives to save or rescue another person. These selfless deeds are the very essence of consideration for others.

There are countless stories of such heroic acts. These individuals aren't necessarily seeking for recognition or accolades, but they deserve the honor they receive just the same. These acts of selfless consideration and heroism, performed by average men and women, often don't make the headlines or the news.

That may be okay. Seeking for recognition is not a hallmark of the Considerate Cow anyway. In fact the Considerate Cow can be found masquerading under several different names. The appellations below were each mentioned several times in my survey. Eventually though I was able to properly identify them as just alternate names for the Considerate Cow. In fact, you may have noticed that the Considerate Cow is the only cow among the eight important cows to only have one name in the chapter heading. That is because I found that this cow goes by *many* different names.

*I believe that the more we love someone the easier it is to know what they want and need.*

Here is an incomplete list:

THE COMFORT COW—Giving comfort is easy in the case of a skinned knee or obvious tear. But recognizing the hidden hurt and reaching out to give solace is a gift that is truly appreciated.

THE UNSELFISH COW—To adequately help someone often requires that we sacrifice our own wants and sometimes needs.

Many times the recipient won't fully know the time and effort expended on their behalf. But the Unselfish Cow doesn't make an accounting or send out bills.

THE LISTENING COW—A listening ear is often the only comfort one may need as they talk through their day, their troubles, and their joys. Taking time to listen, really listen, and then to respond and communicate appropriately is how couples grow close and deepen their relationship.

*Nobody is more in touch with reality than someone who is truly humble.*

THE HUMBLE COW—Nobody is more in touch with reality than someone who is truly humble. People who are humble gratefully acknowledge their strengths and seek for awareness of their shortcomings. Humility is the foundation of all personal and spiritual growth.

THE FORGIVING COW—Holding a grudge is toxic to any relationship. Refusing to forgive is like taking poison and hoping the other person will die. Forgiveness is healing and empowering and allows the giver and receiver to continue to grow together despite past wrongs or injuries.

THE GIVING COW—A thoughtful gift requires . . . well, thought. It requires one to truly think about and understand another person's wishes and desires. Such a gift continues to give long after the actual gift is gone.

The Empathy Cow—It is very liberating to grow in a relationship where you are genuinely able to feel what someone else is feeling. Empathy enables you to know how to best comfort and help the one you love the most. Feeling empathy from another person can take the loneliness or fear out of individual difficulties.

The Even-Tempered Cow—It is hard for a couple to dance when one of the partners is walking on eggshells. An explosive temper has sunk too many love boats. It is a great comfort to know that despite the tempests raging around you, the person you're with will remain calm, cool, and collected.

*It is hard for a couple to dance when one of the partners is walking on eggshells.*

The Self-Improvement Cow— "Why can't you just like me the way I am?" is a common question. It is often asked as an excuse for making little or no effort to change one's behavior or circumstances. And to answer the question, I believe it is possible to *love* someone just as they are. But it can be hard to *like* that person, especially when their behavior is hurtful or inconsiderate. In fact, in most relationships people fall out of *like* long before they fall out of *love*. I believe the desire to improve for the benefit of another person is an act of love and the consummate act of consideration.

The Considerate Cow, in all of its iterations, is the one cow that can bring to its owners the greatest happiness. This cow, freely given, fills one with charity. It is truly about serving and caring for someone as much or more than self. Johnny and Sarita's love for each other will grow more by feeding this cow than any other cow of the eight. Feed it daily!

### CONVERSATIONS BETWEEN JOHNNY AND SARITA

- What was the most considerate act you feel I ever did for you?
- Is there anything I do you find to be inconsiderate?
- Which of the above characteristics of the Considerate Cow am I lacking?
- Do I do anything that irritates you? How would you like me to change?
- If I could do anything for you right now, what would it be?

## QUOTES ON BEING CONSIDERATE

———◆◆◆———

*"True heroism is remarkably sober, very undramatic. It is not the urge to surpass all others at whatever cost, but the urge to serve others at whatever cost."*

—ARTHUR ASHE

*"Being considerate of others will take your children further in life than any college degree."*

—MARIAN WRIGHT EDELMAN

*"The first step to improvement, whether mental, moral, or religious, is to know ourselves - our weakness, errors, deficiencies, and sins, that, by divine grace, we may overcome and turn from them all."*

—TRYON EDWARDS

*"Really big people are, above everything else, courteous, considerate and generous - not just to some people in some circumstances—but to everyone all the time."*

—THOMAS J. WATSON

*"Remember there's no such thing as a small act of kindness. Every act creates a ripple with no logical end."*

—SCOTT ADAMS

# Mad Cow

*"All sin tends to be addictive, and the terminal point of addiction is what is called damnation."*

—*W. H. Auden*

*T*he story goes that one day, Sarita's friend, Fetia, went to the pasture where her husband, Keoni, kept his full herd of nice fat cows. She loved his cows and would often pay them a visit and pat them on the head. On this day, however, she noticed the cows seemed sluggish and had lost some weight. Alarmed, she asked Keoni what was wrong. Keoni assured her everything was fine and said he had just been a little too busy to care for them as well as before. He promised her he would be more attentive in the future.

Fetia returned sometime later and noticed that clearly the cows were wasting away, lying down with no interest in eating or drinking. She looked around to see what could be the source of the problem and saw way over on the corner of the property a small building hidden in some trees. She walked across the lush grass of the pasture, untouched by Keoni's cows, and looked into the little barn. To her surprise, a cow was hidden inside—one she had never seen before and definitely not one of the herd. She could clearly see Keoni had been spending a lot of time caring and tending for this cow and the surrounding structure. However, this cow appeared to be very ill, and its eyes were dark and hollow.

Fetia immediately called the local veterinarian for a consultation. He came out to the farm and examined the lone cow. His diagnosis? Mad Cow Disease—and even more frightening, all of the once healthy cows had also been infected. The vet went back to the hut and confirmed that the stray cow that Keoni had hidden from Fetia was the source of the contamination.

Fetia's head began to swim. When did this happen? Has Keoni had this cow from the beginning or has he picked it up recently? Does it matter? The entire herd is on the line now, and she doesn't know which way to turn. Keoni has brought a deadly illness home to his once fat and healthy cows!

———•◆•———

The Allegory of the Mad Cow, when applied to real life, is one scary tale. Addictions and their consequences are painful and often catastrophic. Johnny and Sarita's relationship and sometimes their very lives, hang in the balance. The persistent spread of addiction and irresponsible behavior in the lives of otherwise good and moral people is causing untold damage in our society. How to deal with this cow in a relationship is not an easy thing to confront, and getting rid of it is sometimes almost impossible. It is certainly difficult if the partner who is thus afflicted refuses to acknowledge their problem or resists seeking help.

*The Allegory of the Mad Cow, when applied to real life, is one scary tale.*

Despite the critical importance of this topic, I do not want to dwell on it at this time except to say that a mad cow in your herd can delay, modify, or destroy your hopes, your dreams, your relationships, your health, and your life. If you have a mad cow, whatever it is, be it drugs, alcohol, infidelity, porn, gambling, or whatever—get help—then starve it, shoot it, or get rid of it any way you can. Eight cows plus one mad cow can, over time, equal no cows. No Johnny. No Sarita. No bull!

# Have a Cow

## CONSCIENCE OVER WILL

*I*n the "Got Cows?" chapter of this book, I indicated that I wanted to know what became of Johnny and Sarita. Well, in my mind there is no question. Their love increased with each passing year as they grew gracefully old together. Johnny was always handsome and robust for his years, and Sarita seemed to age without ever losing a bit of her beauty. Yes, their hair grew white and they had a few wrinkles, but there was an inner peace and joy in their lives that continued to shine in their faces.

People marvel at Johnny and Sarita's mythical love affair to this very day. However, most people don't comprehend that the love and joy they shared is potentially available to everyone. To obtain it requires an offering, though—eight cows, eight critical character traits that make it possible to sustain your relationship. There will be a price to pay, but spending a lifetime together with a loving companion is well worth the work. Times won't always be easy, but having the character necessary to take on life's challenges will help assure that the one you care for the most will always be by your side.

*The gift of one's best self is the noblest gift one can offer another person.*

The Old Testament tells the story of Jacob, who was willing to work seven years for his beloved Rachel. His love for her was such and the anticipation of finally winning her was so exciting that he was moved to say, "the years seemed like a few days." Just like Johnny, he was willing to pay the price for the one he loved.

Our cultures today are quite different. We don't offer cows or indentured servitude for our companions, but we do have the opportunity to present a much greater offering. The gift of one's best self is the noblest gift one can offer another person.

I will admit that for a time I was hesitant to write this book for fear that the very premise of requiring certain character traits or cows before engaging in a serious relationship might make it more difficult for Johnny and Sarita to get together. Men and women today are already waiting longer and longer before thinking about any kind of long-term commitment that might lead to marriage.

The last thing I wanted to do was make getting married even more of a challenge.

In my non-scientific examination of the situation it appeared that the fear and sometimes even casual acceptance of inevitable failure are robbing modern-day Johnnys and Saritas of the will to pursue anything beyond steady dating. I observed that many people, particularly those still reeling from the pain of a failed marriage, doubt that another person can be trusted to bring these character traits to a long-term relationship. But it has been my hope that if we could make this principle of individual character an easy topic to discuss and then do something about, it might allow potential partners to believe that a lasting relationship is actually possible.

*If you truly want to find an eight-cow partner, having eight cows of your own to bring to the relationship will make that possible.*

The more I have thought about it, the clearer it has become to me that if you truly want to find an eight-cow partner, having eight cows of your own to bring to the relationship will make that possible. Having all of your own cows in readiness will give you the confidence to pursue a serious relationship with an attitude of hope and optimism rather than one of fear and pessimism.

My next big fear was everyone would think it was critical to have a full herd of large and healthy cows before pursuing any kind of relationship. That would be a mistake. All of us are in different stages of development. Some of us may be caring for cows that are not fully grown. For example: A young man in college could be nurturing and tending what may be only a Cash Calf. But one could see clearly by his intentions and actions that it will one day be a fully-grown, producing Cash Cow. So it is with all of our herds. All fat and happy cows were once calves. We don't have to disparage or judge harshly here—four fat cows and four healthy calves is still a herd to be proud of.

When I began to see things in this light, my hesitation to put my thoughts into a book went away.

But does it really require eight cows for modern-day Johnny and Sarita to get together? Evidently not. One or two cows seem to be fine. Many people still try to make it work. But they also separate and divorce. Or perhaps they just suffer for years in silent sorrow. I submit that such compromises will leave you with some difficult choices. The only acceptable choice to me, however, and I hope to you, is where both Johnny and Sarita bring all the requisite cows in order to live happily ever after.

As I think about the phrase, "happily ever after," I find myself reflecting back to my childhood dreams and aspirations. Before I ever heard of Johnny Lingo, I dreamed, as do most little girls, of my "knight in shining armor." This metaphor, as I recall, wasn't necessarily a focus on the good looks of the knight—after all he was wearing that bulky helmet. It was however, a focus on his character, his gallantry, his chivalry, his courage, and his goodness. And the fair maiden was a symbol of purity and virtue. Ideally, if a man wanted to win the heart of the fair maiden, he needed to become the knight. And a woman conversely needed to become the fair maiden. Each needed to become a person of good character. Even as a child, the concept seemed so simple to me.

*One's conscience is often characterized as an innate recognition of right and wrong—of good and better—of better and best.*

In my studies beyond childhood I have found that down through the ages—in history, stories, art, and literature—possessing individual character has been championed as one of the most worthwhile pursuits of men and women. Many philosophies teach that such a pursuit is important because your character may be the only thing you can take with you into the next life. I believe we take our relationships with us as well. This concept, for me, makes gathering my cows even more important.

So how does one actually go about getting cows? Well, first of all, I don't think it is rocket science or brain surgery—it may not even be Algebra 101—but it will require a strong desire and some serious honesty—because, ultimately, the question of character is an argument you must win with yourself.

One time-tested way of achieving a certain desirable character trait is by observing the lives of great men and women. The things such persons have done and the behavior they have demonstrated speak volumes on the important role good character plays in all kinds of relationships and in all aspects of society. Learn from their examples and find the fire and drive to do the same as they have done.

In addition to the above, I also believe the power is in us to know what we need to do to become a person of good character. Most religions and philosophical disciplines recognize a basic universal truth. Some describe this truth as God or a Higher Power, while others describe it as the nature of the universe or just the way things are. The general consensus, however, is that this truth is the foundation of goodness and the basis of all positive character traits.

> *Ultimately, the question of character is an argument that you must win with yourself.*

Our individual connection to this power is sometimes described as our conscience. One's conscience is often characterized as an innate recognition of right and wrong—of good and better—of better and best. And when we choose to follow our conscience over our natural desires or "Will," we grow in positive character. We are beginning to gather our cows.

Our Will or Natural Self tends to choose the path of least resistance; it is the easy thing to do. And, subsequently, giving in to these base desires leads to an egocentric life and a character that more easily surrenders when faced with any challenge or opposition. Following our conscience is much more difficult. It requires making a conscious choice to overcome our natural tendencies. It is a form of resistance training that builds the moral and emotional strength of our soul, just as lifting weights builds the muscles of our body. It takes effort to develop a character that does not capitulate to popular opinion, convenience, or selfish desire.

Some people describe the process of obtaining character as an arduous task requiring great thought and introspection. I don't think it is that complicated. To gain character or to obtain any cow described in this book, it may be as simple as engaging in the regular exercise of choosing Conscience over Will—C.O.W. for short. When facing any moral decision, just repeat the phrase *Conscience over Will* in your mind. Follow your conscience and build the muscles of your character.

I have discussed this strategy at length with people from all walks of life. Most agreed that making the wise choice between these two options was the determining factor in the nature of their character. And after each person tried this approach to their daily decisions for a few days they found it was not only an effective tactic but was easy to follow and remember as well.

I am a very visual person so I was thrilled when one of my friends presented me with a graphic representation of "Conscience over Will." It is the same logo you have seen throughout the book.

It depicts a larger C or conscience over a smaller W or will in the background. It also metaphorically portrays the concept of allowing our will to be swallowed up by our conscience. This symbol has become a great reminder for me.

This book has been a lot about getting your cows. And I am going to say it one more time. Have a COW! Choose **Conscience over Will.** Use this basic technique to get your cows. I believe by consistently making this simple choice it is possible for anyone, no matter their age, to become a man or woman of great character. It is never too late.

It also doesn't matter what *stage* of life you are in. If you are single, get your cows before you go to the marriage altar. If you are married and still a few cows short, get the rest of your cows and fall in love with your spouse all over again. And if you've already "got cows" then keep them fat and healthy, avoid any and all mad cows, and always remember the reciprocal assertion, "An eight-cow woman deserves an eight-cow man!"

# About the Authors

## Tracy Lyn Cutler
### by Kurt Dowdle

Tracy Lyn Cutler, like me, hails from Boise, Idaho. I have always known her to be a daring individual, willing to try anything at least once. (Unless it was illegal or went against her morals) Her fearless personality and love of animals led her to work as an animal control officer right out of high school. After graduating from college she eventually settled on becoming an artist, designer, writer, and business owner. She is as comfortable speaking to large groups as she is talking intimately with a close friend.

She is perhaps the most intuitive person I have ever met. She has always been able to sense the feelings and needs of those around her without drawing attention to herself. She is also one of the best listeners I have ever known. These talents were critical as she began this book. She was able to make deep emotional connections with those she interviewed as she was gathering data. She also has a clear vision of what she feels is important and has a desire to help others achieve their own dreams.

## Ty B. Erickson, M.D.
### by Kurt Dowdle

I met Dr. Ty Erickson long before he became a medical doctor. He had graduated from high school at age 16 in Las Vegas, Nevada and was trying to decide on a discipline that would be challenging and rewarding. I remember being in awe of his depth of intelligence even though we were both just teenagers at the time. I had the privilege of working with him on a few projects then.

We lost track of each other for many years until Dr. Erickson was referred to me for a project that required medical input that was consistent with his expertise.

During one busy day I casually mentioned to him the particulars of Tracy's "Cow Book" and that it might be fun to help out. To my surprise, he indicated that the topics scheduled to be covered were very important to him and that he would love to participate. He lent amazing creative direction as well as vital medical and professional expertise that only he could provide.

He holds several medical patents and has traveled the world tutoring other doctors on specialized surgical techniques that he personally developed. Throughout the years, despite his busy schedule, he has volunteered many hours a week in civic and church activities. He lectures regularly, is an avid women's advocate, and has spent countless hours counseling women and couples.

## Kurt Dowdle
### by Tracy Lyn Cutler

Kurt Dowdle was born and raised in Boise, Idaho. I met him first in high school and admired his drive and ambition. He seemed to be a man on a mission. He was active in sports, was a concert violinist in the local symphony, and had already lauched several business ventures.

When I bumped into Kurt later in life, he was a successful business owner and had already participated in eight other book projects where he had acted as either editor or ghost-writer. In our initial conversations he seemed to get where I was coming from with very little explanation. *The Cow Book*, (as we called it) became a three-way collaboration every step of the way. Kurt's insights and experience helped put our thoughts into words in a fun and creative way. He sensed the urgency for the book and helped keep everything on schedule from beginning to end.

To be a part of the eight-cow community for character development and relationship building please visit us on our website at www.eightcow.com. You can also become a fan of "The Cow Book" on Facebook.